Who Needs a Story?

Contemporary Eritrean Poetry in Tigrinya, Tigre and Arabic

Who Needs a Story?

Contemporary Eritrean Poetry in Tigrinya, Tigre and Arabic

Translations by

Charles Cantalupo and Ghirmai Negash
with Others

Edited by

Charles Cantalupo and Ghirmai Negash

Hdri Publishers
June 2005
Asmara

Hdri Publishers
178 Tegadelti Street
House No. 35
P.O.Box 1081
Tel. 291-1-126177
Fax 291-1-125630
Asmara, Eritrea

Who Needs a Story?

Cover Photograph & Design: Lawrence F. Sykes

Cantalupo, Charles, 1951-
Negash, Ghirmai, 1956-
Who Needs a Story? Contemporary Eritrean Poetry in Tigrinya, Tigre and
Arabic /
Charles Cantalupo and Ghirmai Negash.

ISBN 99948-0-008-6

Printed in Eritrea by Sabur Printing Services

CONTENTS

ACKNOWLEDGEMENTS

The editors and translators would like to express their acknowledgements and special thanks to the following persons and institutions. *Who Needs a Story?* is a collaborative effort among Eritrea's People's Front for Democracy and Justice (PFDJ), The Pennsylvania State University and the University of Asmara's Department of Eritrean Languages and Literature. Zemhret Yohannes, the PFDJ's Director of Research and Documentation, initially conceived of the project, and it depended on his inspired, generous and pragmatic support and guidance throughout. The Research and Documentation Center (RDC) – Eritrea provided an elegant and spacious office for us to work in and vital secretarial assistance in typing the Tigrinya and Tigre poems. Elias Amare and Ibrahim Idris Toteel painstakingly went through the final manuscript. The counsel and vision of Lawrence F. Sykes were exemplary. This book has been made possible through generous travel grants from Penn State's Africana Research Center, with additional support from Penn State's Capital College, College of Liberal Arts, Penn State Schuylkill Campus, and Penn State's Department of English and Department of African and African American Studies.

FOREWORD

Conceived and designed to provide students and teachers of African literature and interested readers everywhere – with a concise anthology of Eritrean poetry written in Tigrinya, Tigre and Arabic over roughly the last three decades, this book contains English translations of thirty-six poems by twenty-two contemporary poets. Most of the poets participated in the Eritrean struggle for independence (1961-1991) as freedom fighters and/or as supporters in the Eritrean diaspora. That the majority of the poems present and reflect upon some of the most compelling aspects of this struggle, a young nation's yearning to be born and its aspirations for progress and development may not be surprising.

Since all but a few of the poets of *Who Needs a Story?* – including scholars, professional writers, journalists, social scientists, teachers, actors, theater directors and performers – have never been translated and have never been gathered in a single volume, they have remained unknown, for the most part, outside of Eritrea. However, in Eritrea, as can be said of other African countries, poetry has deep and distinguished historical roots and, although oral or traditional poetry has a longer history than the written, its time for worldwide recognition has finally come. As one of the poets of the book, Reesom Haile, has observed, "Our poetry is not something that has left our tongue and lived in the books for a very long time." But with the completion and publication of this book, contemporary Eritrean poets can be known and enjoyed throughout Africa and the world, much as poets of other countries have achieved worldwide recognition. This result resembles the process through which poets of many different nations have gained an international readership after being previously not widely known: for example, the way that contemporary Eastern European poets were first read widely in

i

the 1970s or South American poets in the 1960s, and without whose influence most contemporary poetry in English and most languages is unimaginable since these poets expressed and explored a sensibility not widely recognized before them. Now is the time for African language poets to be similarly heard, with Eritrean poets as part of the vanguard.

The initiative for the book *Who Needs a Story? Contemporary Eritrean Poetry in Tigrinya, Tigre and Arabic* derives in large part from a literary conference and festival held in Asmara, Eritrea, in January 2000: "Against All Odds: African Languages and Literatures into the 21st Century." From this gathering emerged the historic "Asmara Declaration on African Languages and Literatures," which has since then been translated into a wide range of African languages and other languages worldwide. Addressing its own origins, "The Asmara Declaration" observes that "its initiative...materialized" also out of the *Against All Odds* conference. Moreover, *Who Needs a Story?* is produced in keeping with a number of "The Asmara Declaration's" critical contentions.

Applying the words of the declaration to the aims of this book, *Who Needs a Story?* celebrates "the vitality of African languages and literatures," specifically the languages of Tigrinya, Tigre and Arabic in the contemporary poetry of Eritrea, "and affirms...their potential." Furthermore, *Who Needs a Story?* "note[s]...with pride that despite all the odds against them," the African languages of Eritrea – and Tigrinya, Tigre and Arabic are only three of them – "as vehicles of communication and knowledge survive and have a written continuity of thousands of years." Further corresponding to the mandates of "The Asmara Declaration," the Tigre, Tigrinya and Arabic poetry of *Who Needs a Story?* "take on the duty, the responsibility and the challenge of speaking for" Eritrea and more, embracing people everywhere who use languages and literatures to embody their dreams for a better world. Again in line with the language of "The Asmara Declaration," "the vitality and equality" of Eritrea's languages and their poetry should "be recognized as a basis for the future empowerment" of the Eritrean people. Also, "[t]he diversity of" Eritrea's "languages reflects the rich cultural heritage of" Eritrea and is "an instrument of" Eritrean "unity." Indeed, in the words of the declaration, "[d]ialogue among" Eritrean "languages is essential," and Eritrean "languages must use the instrument of translation to advance communication." Yet again following the declaration, *Who Needs a Story?* would promote "research on" Eritrean "languages" as "vital for their development." Last but not least, the poetry of *Who Needs a Story?* is written in the spirit of reinforcing "what is essential for...the African Renaissance."

Again in harmony with the major themes of the conference's declaration, the poets and the poems of *Who Needs a Story?* are part of a still larger movement to create a pioneering, global and free conversation among languages, literatures and cultures towards discovering and mapping a kind of universal, verbal genome. Translation is a vital part of such an effort. English can be a key to facilitating such a comprehensive, global conversation by enabling rather than disabling communication between and among languages. The reality of English as a global language, when used as a tool of empowerment and not as a substitute for the potential of African languages, establishes it as a common means of translation between and among other languages and literatures, especially those that are marginalized – regardless of their expressive power – apart from the centers of political power. Through translations into a world language like English – as a medium or vehicle from one language to another – different languages of the world can speak to one another and to us as never before. Furthermore, this collaboration empowers them eventually – and this is most important – to translate directly into one another, again a process which occurred at the "Against All Odds" meeting, to take only one example, with the successful translation and staging of Ngugi wa Thiong'o's *I Will Marry When I Want* translated into Tigrinya This translation, by the great Eritrean writer and historian, Alemseged Tesfai, was not directly from the play's original Gikuyu into Tigrinya but through the play's English translation. Yet now the Tigrinya version of *I Will Marry When I Want* has become one of Eritrea's most important contemporary plays. Such a process might be readily duplicated, becoming a renaissance of translations between and among all languages and traditions. Translations from Latin and Greek and into European vernacular languages were a primary force that brought about the European Renaissance or early modern period, leading to an unprecedented development of literatures, cultures and European languages as well as the nations in which they were written, read and spoken. Notwithstanding the important caveat against limiting non-European languages and literatures to European paradigms, translation from an ever-wider sphere of languages, including African languages, can have a similar effect, if we recognize and use the opportunity consciously, and act.

As the translators and editors of this book, we have worked to achieve a qualitative and balanced selection by including what we consider to be a just sampling of the more known and established figures of Eritrean poetry written in Tigrinya, Tigre and Arabic. However, we have also tried to include poems by budding, less established younger poets who, though less well known, are fully engaging and deserve to be included in such a collection. With few exceptions, the poets of *Who Needs a Story?* have published or are preparing for publication one or more books of poetry. We have tried to be fair and impartial by focusing not on quantity but on quality, originality, relevance and these poets' impact on the reading public. Also, we have tried to represent the healthy diversity of voices of which contemporary Eritrean poetry consists, ranging from what might be considered the pre-independence, mainstream poetry of resistance to post-independence – necessarily more innovative and critical – work written by younger independence fighters and poets of the Eritrean diaspora.

Preparing the text, we have been fully aware of the challenges and intricacies of not merely translation but literary translation, which demands mastery of the "first" and "target" languages and also a thorough knowledge of the literature, culture, rhetoric and style of these languages. Translating the Tigrinya, Tigre and Arabic poems of *Who Needs a Story?* has reconfirmed for us the canonical wisdom that any kind of translation – literal to "free" – is limited in what it can accomplish. Too much adherence to formality and exactness can result in a text that is unreadable, artless and even meaningless. An overly interpretative translation that is "imitative" merely in spirit clearly undermines and even patronizes authenticity. Literary allusions, site-specific references, symbolism, imagery, prosody, puns, jokes, aphorisms, irony and so much more can defy translation to and from any language. Furthermore, translation, especially literary translation, is a continuum, be it within a single language, between two languages or among many. From the writer working on his or her own literary manuscript – almost by definition a kind of very private language – to the translator working between two or more different languages, the attention given to style, content, rhetoric, genre, reader or audience, tradition and innovation must be similarly intense if the language of the result – the poem, the play, fiction or nonfiction – is as all literature should, to delight and teach.

Therefore, attempting to avoid extremes and as many problems as possible, we have tried to create translations which adhere to the original while simultaneously attempting a broader kind of cultural translation whenever it was required to be faithful to the beauty and apparent intent of the original. In such instances, haunted by the infamous, stinging conundrum in Italian – *traduttore / traditore*, meaning the translator is a traitor – we have tried as translators to be traders, offering as fairly and equally as possible, one kind of cultural artifact for another. We have shared in the belief that individual languages, poets and poems have never existed solely unto themselves but are like bridges, currents, germs, dust, liquids and atmospheric conditions as they move through continents, boundaries, islands, oceans, the light of the sun and the stars, in between and among themselves.

Many people have worked together to make this book. Their various contributions at different stages of the project have been enormous. Yet throughout the process, our aim has been to make translations into English that are as close as possible to the essence yet which embody the deepest sensibilities of Eritrean poetry as found in the poems we have selected. This process unfolded as follows.

In the summer of 2002, Charles Cantalupo traveled to Eritrea for a first meeting with many of the poets, Ghirmai Negash, and other experts of Eritrean literature, and discussed what and whom the book might include. Based on these discussions, he found the prospect of a book of translations of contemporary poetry written in several of Eritrea's languages undeniably attractive. In 2003 over sixty Tigrinya, Tigre and Arabic poems were translated and evaluated for their quality and accessibility to determine the actual feasibility of the project. Rahel Asgedom and Nazreth Amlessom, both lecturers in the English department at the University of Asmara, made the first translations of about half of forty Tigrinya poems which would be short-listed for inclusion in the book. Adem Saleh, an Eritrean television journalist, and Desale Bereket, a columnist for the newspaper, *Haddas Eritrea*, and a senior student in English at the University of Asmara, made the first drafts of poems in Tigre. Ghirmai Negash, chair of the Department of Eritrean Languages and Literature at the University of Asmara, coordinated and supervised this first phase of the translations in Tigrinya and Tigre, translated the second half of the Tigrinya poems, read all of the translations and made changes for accuracy and readability. The widely respected and senior journalist, Said Abdulhay, with whom Charles Cantalupo also met in 2002 to discuss the prospect of the book, accepted the responsibility of coordinating the translation of poems in Arabic. Since the Arabic poems' inclusion in the book was considered essential from the start, they were sent for translation to *Mekki for Translating & Printing*, an international translation office in Beirut, Lebanon, which provided excellent translations of the Arabic poems' first drafts in English.

Receiving the first drafts in English of all of the translations by the end of 2003, Charles Cantalupo began working on their second drafts. Checking for linguistic accuracy and reading and rewriting the work as an English-speaking poet, literary critic and scholar, he produced a complete book manuscript, which he then returned to Ghirmai Negash, who read and commented upon it.

At the end of the summer of 2004, Charles Cantalupo and Ghirmai Negash met in Asmara for the final stage of the project. Basing their discussion of the poems on Ghirmai Negash's comments, they began an engaging, at times intense yet always pleasurable dialogue about the poems in Tigrinya. In addition, they both consulted with Said Abdulhay and Mussa Aron, whose knowledgeable and insightful comments on the Arabic and Tigre poems respectively, along with their English translations, resulted in a similarly happy and productive process of literary collaboration. With the inspired guidance and the absolutely critical corrections of the text provided by Ghirmai Negash, Charles Cantalupo then wrote the final version of the book.

This final version required that the number of poems and poets whom we had originally planned to include had to be cut. Deciding on which poems and which poets to cut was extremely difficult. We wanted to include more poets and more poems by them than we had space for. Of course, we desired to present only the best and the most representative of contemporary Eritrean poets. Moreover, many of the poems we cut were too obviously imitations of these poets' work. We also cut poems that seemed too cryptic or opaque in their translation, although they could be wonderful in the original.

After careful consideration and much discussion, we finally made a decision to include only written poetry and not Eritrean oral poetry, which has a long and rich tradition, and which is still very important and pervasive in Eritrea. An objection to this critical decision would surely be just. We firmly believe that the depth, breadth and high quality of Eritrean oral poetry warrant a translation project and an edition of its own. Yet we foresee a mapping of the Eritrean verbal genome to include all of Eritrea's languages as well as their performative and literary dimensions, with *Who Needs a Story?* making only several steps in this noblest of endeavors.

Charles Cantalupo   **Ghirmai Negash**

Meles Negusse

We Miss You, Mammet

Mammet, where are you?
We miss the way your rhythms
Balanced truth and beauty
In the word of a thousand songs
Pulsing in and out of you
And containing love so strong
It mastered all our art.

Among the hills and cliffs
You ruled with your poetry
Not a single riff
Of your melodies remain
But only mourners
All too ready to say
Mammet is in her grave

Along with her rhymes.
Poetry is declared dead.
Still we crave
Seeing and hearing you again
And there must be a way
For the mysterious power
Of your voice to return

If merely for a moment
To recall your spirit
And sound of joy
To the poetry of today,
Even if you're buried

ማመት ናፈቝናኪ

ማመት ናፈቝናኪ ማመት ስኒ ረጸ
ጥበብኪ ግርማዊ ኢንታ ዘይወጸ
ማመት ናፈቝናኪ ናፈቝናዮ ግጥሚ
ተምጽእዮ ናዕታ ስምዒት ዝመሟ
ማመት ጐይታ ጥበብ
ደጉልኪ ንፍቝሪ
ግጥምን መዛይምቲን
አብ ትሕቲ አጻድፍ
አብ ትሕቲ ሽንጭሮ
ግብአቶም አዊጆኪ
አኲብኪ ቀባር
ቀኣሪ ምስኮነና ምእንቲ ክንፍሕር
ቃናኺ ግን የለን ካበይ ክንፍሕትሮ?
ስለዚ ናፈቝና ድምጽኺ አስምዒ
ስነ-ጽሑፍ የለን ተባሂሉ ብወግኒ
አሰኹ እንዶ በሊ ማመት ተቓልቀሊ
እንተስ ብመለኮት ወይ'ውን ብፍሉይ ሓይሊ
መልአኽኪ ስደዲ ካብ ሰማይ ንምድሪ
ማመት ናፈቝናዮ ወጀሂ ቃና ግጥሚ
ዕምቆት ስኢ.ንናሉ ኲሉ ናይዚ ሎሚ
ወሲድክዮ ዲኺ ምስጢር ናይቲ ጥበብ
ነፊሩ ምሳኺ አውጺኡ መንገብገበ
ዋላስ አጽቂጡ'ዩ ብድሕሬኺ ኣቝቢጹ
'ቲ ምህር ረብሪቡ ሓንጺጹ ሓንጺጹ
ግደፊ'ባ ማመት መስጣ'ለዎ ጥበብ
አባና አብ አሕዋትኪ አይትግበሪ ዓገብ

And rest in peace, only
To inspire heaven
With your feeling,
While writers waste away
To nothing, silenced
And forever abandoned
Unless, for the sake of art,
You can fall from the sky,
Mammet, and open our hearts
With your secret poetry's sacred key.

ወይ ተመለሲ ንራይሞክ ክትሕረዪ
ወይ ድማ ካብ ሰማይ መፍትሕ ደርብዪ!

Wild Animals

What are you running away from?
Where would you like to be?
Forget your jungle
And come to the city.

Not even one bush remains
Back there. Enough thunder
And the ground always shaking.
Here you can take it easy.

Look, the gate opens.
Leave your fear outside.
Welcome.
Young or old, women or men –
No one should be denied
The comforts of civilization.

Or has the jungle
Already seen it come,
Leaving mines instead of trees
And trading you sulfur
For the breath of freedom?
Better take the city instead

And let that wild man
Sniffing blood
Live the way you used to
But not any more –
Eating his own kind
Dead or alive.

He can have your place.

እንስሳ ዘገዳም

ንምንታይ ትሃድሙ
　　ናበይ'ዩ እዚ ህድማ
ግደፍዎ በረኻ ንዑ ኝኸተማ
'ቲ ትድቅስሉ ቆጥቋጥ ተቦርቀኍጄ
ሒም ሒዋታ በዚሑ ከውሒ ተነኞኒጄ
ንዑ'ምበር እተዉ
　　ክንከፍቶ ካንሸሉ
　　እንታይ ጌንኩም ትሰግኡ
　　እቲ ዘሎ አበይ አሎ?
ምስ ሸማግለ አረገውቲ
ምስ ቄልዓ ሰበይቲ
ክትነብሩ ምእንቲ
　　እተዉ ንውሻጠ
　　የለን ዋላ ሓደ።
እቲ ትነብሩሉ ብሰብ ተባሒቱ
ፈዕ ትብልሉ ጨካ ቃሬት ሸቲቱ
　　ገረብ መሲልኩም ብረት ከይትረግጹ
　　ከተማ ብሃጉ በረኻ ጭበጹ
　　　　አብቲ ናትኩም ቦታ
　　　　ከም መተካእታ
　　ሰብ አሎ፥ ሰብ አራዊት፥
　　ፈን ፈን ይብል ደም ይሸትት
ንዑ ቆይሩና ንሕና ክንሸፍቶ
ሰብ ንሰብ ክበልዓ ሕግኹም ክንብሕቶ።
　　ለውጢ'ኮ ጽቡቕ'ዩ!
እተዉ ከተማ፥ ጤሎ-በጊዕ ሓረዱ
ተዓረጄ ድማ ነበሪ ጤለበዱ
አንበሳ አይትግዓር ስቕ ኢልካ አመሓድር
ተመን'ውን አይትንከስ ምስ ርግቢት ሕደር
　　ወኻርያ ትም በሊ
　　ምስ ማንቲለ አዕልሊ
　　　　አይትመናጨቲ
　　　　ተሳኒኹም ኪዱ።
ንሕና'ውን ክንለምዱ እቲ ናትኩም መንበር
እናተበላላዕና በረኻ ክንሰፍሮ

Come to the city and thrive.
Hey tiger and deer,
Try a little peace.
Lion, lose the roar.
You can rule with justice.

Snake, you don't have to bite
The dove when you kiss.
And fox, forget the deceit
When you talk with the rabbit.

In the city we all get along.
The war of every man
Against every man belongs
In the jungle.

Leave it behind you.
Take the leap.
The change will be good.
Try my bed to sleep.

እንስሳ ዘገዳም ኣብ ዓራት ደቀሱ
ሰብ ኣራዊት ይኹን ንሸኹም ንገሱ!
ተሓዲግኩም ቦታ ኣይትሸቍረሩ
ክፎማ እተዉ ሕጊ ተቐይሩ'ዩ!

Isayas Tsegai

I Am Also a Person

When I saw the world didn't care
If I was stripped of everything,
Even my dignity,
And beaten like a slave
Less than human,
I lost all sense of peace except in saying
I am also a person. I'm an Eritrean.

Clenching my teeth in the cold,
I had to embrace suffering.
Hunger was all I had.
The wind wanted my bones.
With death so close,
I wished I was never born
But I still said, *I am also a person.*

I left my home
Because it abandoned me.
I left my stream
Because I would have drowned.
I left.
I couldn't bear the burden
Of my birthplace gone:

The crumbled barn
And livestock disappeared,
The yard smelling only of dust,
Nothing to make into bread
Because there was no harvest;

ስብ'የ

ኤርትራዊ ስብ'የ እነ'ውን
ሰብ ኢኺ ኢለያ ንነብሰይ - ስነይ ናኺሰ።

ብስስዐ ተገፊዐ ህይወት ምስ ረሓቐት፡
ሰላም ጠፊኣ ዓመጽ ምስ ነገሰት፡
ክብረይ ተደፊሩ ግዙእ ምስ ኮንኩ፡
ሰብ ኣይኮንካን ምስ ተበሃልኩ - ምስ ተረገጽኩ፡
ሰብ ኢኺ ኢለያ ንነብሰይ - ስነይ ናኺሰ!

ኣብ ጨራሪ ለይትታት፡
ንፋስ ክሽብብ ብናህሪ፡
ንኣካላተይ ክድንድኖ፡
ንሕሰመይ ክሓሪ።

ጥምየተይ ክዛይድ፡
ምፍጣረይ ከጽልኣኒ፡
መቓብር ኑረቤተይ፡
ሞት ክትቀርበኒ፡
ሰብ ኢኺ ኢለያ ንነብሰይ - ስነይ ናኺሰ።

ቤተይ ገዲፈ - ቤተይ ምስ ገደፈኒ፡
ሩባይ ገዲፈ - ጽፍሒ ማይ ዓሚቚኒ፡
ዓደይ ገዲፈ - ሓይሊ ማይ ምስ ተጸዕነኒ።

እቲ ቀኑዕ ነገፋ፡
ቆጽ ተጐንበዮ፡
ጥሪት ሃዲመን
ደምብ ሓመድ-ሓመድ ጨነዮ።

እንታይ ክስንክቶ'ቲ መንጎ፡
እኽሊ ዘየለ ዝጒጐን፡
መልአክ ሞት ድርቂ እናጠጠየ፡
መረረ ክውሽኽኒ እናተንየየ፡
ሰብ ኢኺ ኢለያ ንነብሰይ - ስነይ ናኺሰ።

10

Nothing but drought ahead
Or the angel of death;
Nothing but one horror
Pouring over another.

Clenching my teeth, I said it again:
I am also a person. I remembered
Birds in the swaying trees,
Wild animals, buzzing bees,
How clouds gathered to rain,

The rhythm of the sea
And music in the stream –
They were our dominion and legacy.
We ate and dressed well,
Living and sleeping in peace
And devoted to good work.
I loved this country.

I wanted it back.
If I endured
I would get my reward.
Peace, progress and freedom
Began with those words.
Clenching my teeth, I had to tell myself.
I am also a person. I'm an Eritrean.

አዕዋፍ እናበረራ፥ አናህብ እናኾለሉ፥
አግራብ እናፉጸልጸለ፥ አራዊት እናዘለሉ፥
ደበናታት ተአኪፒዞም ክፍንጥሑ - ዝናብ
ክፈጥሩ፥
ባሕሪ እናወፈረ ወሓይዝ እናጉረሩ።

ሰባት ክመልክዎም፥ ክዓብይሎሙ ክብገሱ፥
ጽቡቕ ክበልዑ፥ ጽቡቕ ክለብሱ፥
ህይወት ክሪኡ ልዋም ክድቅሱ፥
ጽቡቕ ከዛይዱ ንጽቡቕ ክቃለሱ - ርእየ፥
ሰብ ኢኺ ከአ ኢለያ ንነብሰይ - ስነይ ኻሰ።

አነ'ውን...... ሰብ!
ጽቡቕ ዝደሊ ብጽቡቕ ዝቘንእ
ዕብየት ዝደሊ ሰላም ዝናፍቕ

ዕድለይ ገፊልጥ....ዘውስን በዓል ሓንጎል፥
ጸቕጢ ዘይቅበል በዓል ሃገር፥
በዓል ሃገር...... ኤርትራዊ...... ሰብ'የ!
ሰብ ኢኺ ኢለያ ንነብሰይ..........
ሰብ ምኻን'የ ጻማ ገድለይ!

Lamentation

I'm feeling overwhelmed by death.
If there is no life without it
Better to have never been born.
Why make any effort at all
If death swallows everything?
Why even ask the question if
Nothing answers but death – death with
No chance of justice or freedom

And death essential as water
Quenching everyone? The dead
Sons and daughters of Adal
And Denden and all the heroes
Finally at home in their graves
Know only one true answer if
I ask, "Is this the promised end?"

I don't know what to do or say.
"Victory to the Masses!" or
"Victory to Me!" What's the point?
I thought I knew which way was best
But now I want to run away
And hide in a monastery

Because I remember my friend.
I see his blood, bones and spirit.
His fight and his struggle echo
Yet with a profound sense of peace
Ordering me everyday:
"Get up…you can do it…you can…."
Still, I want to forget this voice

13

ደጉዓ ህልው

እንታይ ኢዩ'ዚ ሰብ መዋቲ ዝፍጠር፡
ሓደው ከይተወልደ ምስ ግሩዝ ዘይጽንበር፡
ሓደው ስለግብሩ ኣብ ክልተ ዘይምቀል፡
ምንባር'ዶ ዘይምንባር ብርትዒ ዘይምለስ፡
ፍትሒ ዘየውጽእ እዚ መግዛእቲ ትንፋስ።

እዚ ወዲ ኣዳል ወዲ ደንደን ሙማት፡
ለካ ንበዓል ሩሕ መቘናንያ 'ዛ ሕልፈት፡
ተራ ከም ማይ ኮይኑ ንኹሉ ዘዐንግል፡
ሓባእ ጅግና ከኣ'ዩ ገሊኡ መቓብር፡
እንታይ'ሞ ኣሎ'ዩ ክበሃል ካብ ሓቂ ዝጭክን።

ገለን እናነበረ "ዓወት ንዓይ!" ዳዊቱ፡
ገለን እናሓለፈ "ዓወት ንሓፋሽ" ማህሌቱ።
እንታይ'ዩ'ዚ ባሪ ገለመለ ኣሕባሩ፡
ጎመዳ እንዶ ኹኑ ሓንገርቲ መትከሉ፡
ገዳመይ ክስፍር ክኸውል ካብ ገኸሩ።

ዓጽም-ደሙ ኣብ ኣዒንተይ እናሰረበ፡
መልአክ ጽላሎቱ ናብ ህላወ እናቐረበ፡
ጨናግር ተግባራቱ መቓልሕ እናሃበ፡
ቅሳነት መንፈሱ'ሞ ውርሻ'ንድዩ ሚስጥሩ፡
ገዳም ዘስፈረኒ ዝኸውለኒ ካብ ገኸሩ።

መሬት ተመጕታ ባሕረይ'ዩ ካብ በለት
"ጽንዓት!" ካብ መለሰ ልመና ሰማያት፡
ዕድሉ'ኮ ኣይነብረን ብስለተ'ዩ እቲ ሞት፡
እኔ መን ኮይነ'የ መትበሩ ዘይቅነት፡
ቀልቢ መን ዓዲገ ዓለመይ ከቅምት።

ከም'ኡ ተበዚሓም ልቢ ዝልቦም፡
ከም'ኡ ተበዚሓም ስራሕ ዝጣእቶም፡
ከም'ኡ ተበዚሓም ኤርትራ ዝሃዮም፡

14

If only the land would let me
Instead of repeating, "It's you.
Your choice. Your strength.
Your sacrifice. This is your chance."

How do I refuse this mantle
Laid on like a form of worship
And like the only eyes I have

To see if others – if I – have
His heart and if we work as hard
And can dream like him of a land
Of more than death and of freedom?
What other calling can there be
To real peace, the kind that I might
Find in a monastery if
It meant not escape but praise for

His love pouring on us like rain,
His voice so tender in the grass,
His death giving life to the land
And birth to deep satisfaction
Within our nation – a holy chant
I would join indeed if it meant
Forgetting the pain of his death.

I can neither see nor touch him,
But how do I forget feeling
Constantly and at the same time
The power of life and death identical
To him and looking in my eyes
From beyond the stars, asking if
I'm dead, alive or in between?

ባዕለይ ደፊነዮ ስለምንታይ እንበር፡
ዓለም ሕቖይ ሂባ ገዳመይ ዘይስፍር።

ዓሚቝኈ ኖኽሩ ከም ዝናብ እንተወሪዱ፡
ለምለም ድሃዩ ኣብ ነግሒታት እንተዓሪዱ፡
ህይወት ሃገሩ ብሞቱ እንተሰሚሩ፡
ሞቱ ብህይወት ህዝቡ እንተቐኣጸልጺሉ፡
ገዳም ኣብጽሑኒ ክእለ ካብ ገኽሩ።

ንሱ!....ኣብ ኩሉ'ዩ ዘሎ ዘይድህሰስን ዝጭበጥን
ሓይለ መንፈስ ሓይለ ህልውን መዋትን፡
ክንዮ ከዋኽብቲ ርሒቑ ነዒንተይ ይቐርበን፡
እንታይ ክበሃልየ ዝርእን ዘይርእን፡
ገዳመይ ስፈረ ክልቲኡ ዘይስእን።

ንሱ!......ድምጺ ኣዕዋፍ ኣይሰምዐን፡
መኣዛ ዕምባባታት ኣይሸተተን፡

ዓልመት እናሓሊኸ ሃገር'ዩ ዘሚሩ
ክስጣሕ እንተሪኤ ንሞት ገጹ ከሊኡ፡
ገዳም እንተሰፈርኩ ቀረባ እንድዩ ናብኡ።

ንዘየሎ ካብ ዘልዕል፡
ምስ ዘይህውሉ ካብ ዝነብር፡
ብገኽሩ ካብ ዝልሎ፡

If I could forget this feeling
Hiding in a monastery,
He would still not hear birds singing.
He would still not smell spring flowers.

He would still chew sulfur and fall
Dead for the sake of our nation,

Though I would pray to be the soil
Of the shrine and hold his body,
Devote my words to his absence,
Live without touching or seeing,
Burn only with his memory
And hope his heirs will learn to thrive
On his dreams still very alive.

ተካእቲ ብዝሓለይ ሕልምታቱ፡ ትፈትሑ፡
ገዳመይ ክሰፍር ማሓሉለይ ብኡ።

18

Solomon Tsehaye

The Tithe of War

I struggled in battle,
Won the war
And earned a rest.
My bones ploughed
The ground of peace.

It flowered and multiplied –
Watered with my sweat,
Fed with my flesh
And sweetened by my marrow.
The harvest was good.

Now I could sleep, content
With a blanket of earth,
Bushes for friends,
A mattress of dust
And a pillow of stones,

Except my spirit groans
When I hear you crying,
As you ululate and sing.
And when I see you crying
As you dance so proud.

I hear you, mother,
And I see your loved ones
Like a little wheat remaining
In the gleaned fields,

መባእ

መጉተ ረቲ0
·ⁱ ዋጊአ አድሚ0፡፡

ተኽለይ ተኽሊ ራህዋ
ተኽሊ ስናይ ተኽሊ ጸጋ፣
ብጭኾይሮ ዓጽመይ ተኾስኩሳ
ብመስኖ አንጉ0ይ ተርኪሳ፣
ዓምቢባ - ነብስ ስጋይ ተመጊባ
ፈርያ - ደም ርሃጸይ ስትያ፡፡

ዓስቢ ጻማይ ስላም ሐፈስ
ልበይ ዓሪፉ አስተርሕየ ደቂስ፣
ኮበርታይ ጨርሒ ጎረቤተይ ቆጥቋጥ፣
ደጊም መቂሩኒ ዕጨ - እምኒ ምጽቃጥ፣
ሐመድ መንጸፈይ ፍርናሽ ጥዒሙኒ
አካ ለስለስለይ መተርአሰይ እምኒ!

ዘተክዝ እንደሞ እህህታ ስሚ0
እህህታ አደየ ካብ ልቢ 'ተጎስ0!
ዓዓሊልኪ ትነብዒ
ጨጨራርኪ ትነብዒ
ደደሪፍኪ ትነብዒ
ስሳዕሲዕኪ ትነብዒ
ተሓቢንኪ ኸኣ ትነብዒ፣
ክልተ አምሳል አብ ሓደ አካል፡፡

ብጸተይ፣ ከም ካብ ዓጺድ ቀሪም ዝተረፉ፣
ብጸተይ፣ ከም ካብ ብሱል ጥረ ዝወጹ
ገጽኪ ይሕልዉ'ለዉ'ም ክትነብዒ ይስቀቑ
ንዕአም ሕሰብለይ ምትራፍም ከይጸልኡ፡፡

ከምቲ ትምኖንዮ መባእ ንጽድቂ
መባእ እንድየ አነስ መባእ ስለሓቂ፣

20

Or like a few raw seeds
 When there's nothing left to eat.
Constantly hearing you cry
And seeing you in pain,
They think, *should we have survived?*
How will they go on?

Who gives a tithe
And asks for it back?
Mother, I paid it,
For you and all our freedom
Not to cry but live.

እመና ከቡር'ዩ ናጽነት ዋግኡ
መባእ'ውን ንቡር'ዩ ከይምለስ ቆፈኡ።

Angessom Isaak

Freedom's Colors

I saw a color
Unbelievably bright
And like a powerful wind
Encompassing the sky
Mirrored across the sea
And pouring freedom
All around me.

I remember it again –
The one and only true
Color of freedom:
I never saw such white,
Such red like blood,
Yellow to pale all yellows
And blue beyond God's grace.

But freedom shines less now.
The colors run into each other.
I can't see one color alone.
I don't know why,
And never could I have imagined
My vision ending like this: black,
Blacker than a crow's eye.

Whether my vision has changed
Or if I have become smarter –
Again I don't know, but I don't see

ሕብሪ ናጽነት

እዚ. ሕብሪ ናጽነት፡
ቅድሚ ናጽነት ይደምቅ፡፡
ሓይሉ ከም ሓይሊ ሰማያት፡
ንውቅያኖስ ንባሕረ-ቀላያት፡
ብሰፈሑ ጎሽድን ...
ዝመልእ፤
ዘሀንጢ. ድማ ...
አብ ካልአት ምርኣዩ ዘቕንእ፤
ሸዑ...
ሸዑ አዝዩ ድሙ፝ቕ ሕብሪ ነይሩም፡
ከም'ቲ ኪኹኖ አለዎ'ለ ዝበሀነ፡፡
ከይፈልጥክዎ...
ሓደ ካብ መሰረታውያን ሕብርታት እህቦ፡
ይደምቀለይ ከአ ነበረ፡፡
ንሱ ዝጸዕደወ፡
ካብ ቀይሕ ዝቆይሐ፡፡
ካብ ብጫ ዝበጨወ፤
ፍጹም ሰማያዊ ... ከም ሰማያት ዝኸበደ፡፡
እሞ ሕጂ. ድአ ስለምንታይ'ዩ?
ድምቀት ሕብሩ ነክዩ፡
ዝተዋሰበ ዝመስለኒ፡
ምርድኡ ዘሸግረኒ፡፡
እቲ ቀደም...
አካል ሕብሪ ናጽነት ዘይመስለኒ፡
ጸሊም ከአ አለዎ፤
ካብ ኺኽ ዝጸለመ ... ካብ ክፋል ጸሊም ዓይኒ፡፡
ምርኣየይ ድዩ ጸቢቡ?
ወይ'ስ ልቦናይ እናሓደረ በቑሉ ...
ካልአት ሕብርታት አለልዩ፡፡
ከም ዙረት ዓይኒ ነፋሒቶ ዙረት ዓይነይ፡
ሰለስተ ሚእትን ሱሳን ዲግሪ እንተዘኾኑለይ፤
ንዝገጠመኒ ሕብሪ፡
ንዘውዓለኒ መዓልቲ

24

Freedom in one color only,
As I roll my eyes like a chameleon,
Becoming whatever color I see
To survive.
I experience freedom
As more than one color.
I understand freedom
As more colors than one –
More than I have ever seen,
More than I have ever heard,
And more than I can explain.

ሡሲላ ክትሓድር ... ምመሃርክዋ ንነብሰይ።
ከመይ ...?
እዚ ሕብሪ ናጽነት ሓበጀረዋይ'ዩ፤
ከም'ቲ እዝኒ ብምስማዕ ...
ዓይኒ ድማ ብምርኣይ አይመልእን'ዩ።

Fessahazion Michael

Naqra

At dead center
The sea
Has no fish,
No ships, no storms and no tides
But an island –
Naqra!

All that the storms and tides
And the surrounding water
Reveal
Is desolation
With nothing
To keep a human
Or anything alive
Except the unreachable
Stars above and fish below.

The sea has nothing to show
But Naqra,
Lonely in the distance,
Graceless,
Smelling only of death
And hell.

You know the history –
How many of our people
Fighting for our country
And imprisoned there,
Succumbed in despair
On Naqra.

ናኹራ

ዓሳ ወይስ መርከብ
ማዕበል'ዩ ወይስ መርበብ
እቲ ኣብ ማእከል ባሕሪ ዝርከብ

   ደሴት ኢያ መሬት
   ብማይ ባሕሪ ዝተኸበት
   ናይ ማዕበል ጐረቤት

ጽውጽው ትብል በረኻ
ሰብ ዘይርከባ ኣእዋኻ
መግቢ የብላን ጠሚኻ

   ብላዕሊ ከዋኽብቲ ሰማይ
   ብታሕቲ ዓሳታት ማይ
   ብዘይካ'ዚ የብላን ዝርኣይ

ናይ ዓሳታት ትርኢት
ኣብ ጽምዋ ዝቖመት
ናኹራ እትብሃል ደሴት

   ኩሉ ይፈልጠ ዛንታኣ
   ኣብ ሃገርና ቦታኣ
   ናይዛ ደሴት እዚኣ

መሰል ህዝቢ ዝበሉ
ንማዕርነቶም ቃልሶም ዝኸፈሉ
ምእንቲ ሓርነት እተጋደሉ

   ብጸላኢ ዝተታሕዙ ሓርበኛታት
   ተኣሲሮም ተወስዱ ናብዛ ደሴት
   ናብ ናኹራ ንስቅያት

ናኹራ፣ ማእሰርቲ ሓርበኛታት
ናኹራ፣ ናይ ጀጋኑ መሕየሪት
ቦታ ኣውያት፣ ደሴት ስቅያት።።

28

Ribka Sibhatu

Abeba

Abeba, my flower from Asmara . . .
Measured and subtle
As her makeup
And her finely drawn eyes –
She spoke like poetry.

The food her family sent
To prison everyday
Arrived as usual
The day her grave was dug.
I heard her cry.

Later that night
I also heard
The prison guard
Summon her out
And the shot.

She lives in my dreams
And refuses to leave,
Knowing all my secrets
And never letting me rest.

Before she died
She wove a basket
Inscribed "for my parents" –

Abeba, my flower from Asmara . . .
Who never blossomed.
My cell-mate.

29

እቡብይ

......እበባ ጓል አስመራ
እብ ሓዝሓዝ ሰፈራ፤

አየወ... እቡብ ቅጭን፤
ዘረባእ ኵሉ ብዕቅን፡
ከም ዓይንን ኵሕልን፤
ሓደ ሸምን መልክዕን፡፡
ምስጢር ሞት ሓዚላ፡
ጋህሳ እናኸዐዱቴሳ፡
ንዓለም ተእወየሳ፡

ሰደደት... አገልግል ሕምባሻ ደይብሳ፡፡

ለይቲ-ምድሪ ካብ ጐድነይ፡
ብመቘኅሕ ተመንዘዐት እቡብይ፡፡
....
ትመሳለስ አብ ሕልመይ፡
ቀትሪ-ቀትሪ ትገድፈኒ በይነይ፡፡
ካብ አበየት ካባይ ምፍላይ፤
ሒዛታ'ሳ መልሲ ሕቶይ፤

"መዘክርታ ንወለደይ"
ትብል አገልግል እቡብይ
አምጽኡለይ፤
ናይ'ታ ከይዓምበበት ድዓረባ
እቡብ መተኣስርተይ፡፡

30

Saba Kidane

Growing Up

My kid is growing up –
  I trust him to baby sit
  And run errands around the block.
I see him growing up –
  He takes messages
  When someone calls
  And can make his own snacks.
He's getting to be that age –
  Measuring, he knows how much.
  Sometimes he beats me at math.
He's growing up –
  He knows what I have to do
  And even takes care of our pets.
  Seeing my brushes and paintings
  Now he remembers, "Don't touch."
My kid is growing up.

ዓንኬል ፋሕዮ

ነቢዙለይ!
    ሓብቴ'ኂ የጽንሕ
    ሰጥ ኢሉ ይለኦኸ
ነቢዙለይ!
    ቴለፎን'ኂ ይቕበል
    ፍሪጅ ከፊቱ ይዕንገል
ነቢዙለይ!
    ፋል ምስፋር ከኢሉ
    ሕሳብ ከይተጋገየ ይኣቱ
ነቢዙለይ!
    አጣል ውዒሉ
    ቆጼራ የጽንሓለይ
ነቢዙለይ!
    ብብራሽ ከም ዘይጽወት
    ስእሊ ከም ዘይጽየቕ ፈሊጡለይ
ነቢዙለይ!

32

Go Crazy Over Me

Come here.
I want to pray for you.
Go crazy over me.

Don't act like you don't care.
Take off those clothes.
What do you have to lose?
I'm a free soul,
Never afraid to laugh.
Compassion lets me play
A slave or a king,
Happy to give away
All that's given to me.

What do you say?
Go crazy. It's ok.
Love is the only thing to do
And I know the way.

I don't want to complain
That water is too thin
And my shadow has run away,
Leaving me with lies,
Alone, bitter, vain
And going crazy too,
Since you're not crazy about me.

But don't worry.
My prayer is not really true.
If you really went crazy
I wouldn't know what to do.

ተጸለልለይ'ባ

ክጽልየልኪ'የ
ክትጸድቂ ኣብ ዓለመይ
ክትህልዊ ኣብ ጎነይ

ጨርቆኺ ደርቢኺ
ዘይምግዳሸ ለቢሰኪ
ናብራይ ምዉቕ'ዩ
ዕድመይ ንደንጋጺ
ንደላዩ ነብሲ

ተደልየ እባሪ ተደልየ እንግስ
ከም ቃሕታይ እስሕቕ
ዝተለገሰለይ ነይበቕኻ

ተጸለልለይ'ባ
ንሱ'ውን ጽድቂ'ዮ
ኣይትጠራጠሪ
ፍቕሪ ምሽ ኩሉ'የ

ንዒ በሊ ከተሓሕዘኪ
ጀምሪ ኢኺ
"ማይ ቀጠን በሊ
ጽላሎተይ ሓሳዊ
ገዲፍኒ ነቢዙ
ከየርከበኒ ሓንጊዱ"

እንታይ ኣለዋ ኢዶ ግዲ
እዚ ምቁር ጽላል
ዓርኒሩኒ ብዘይ ናትኪ ህላወ
ንዘይትጽለልለይ ድየ ተጸሊለ

ኣይ ምኻን ከኣ ንሰለይ ግደፍዎ
ደሓር ከኣ ናይ ብሓቂ እንተጌርክዮ
ብታሕጓስ መን ክሓውዮ?

34

"Your Father"

Propped on the sidewalk
With a few coins near her legs
And a child wrapped in the folds
Of her scarf worn to shreds,
She holds out her hand in the cold.
The modest bend of her head
Says she doesn't want to beg
But she must to feed her son.

Left on her own when he was born,
She cried and cursed her fate.
Where to go? What to do?
She had no other choice – the street –
But he went with her, too,
And now she sees he has grown.
"Let me show you," he says,
Putting out his hand to play.

At first it makes her laugh
To see him imitate
Her begging in his own way.
She's not totally hopeless
And can accept who she is
As long as she has him.
But then it hits her: what if
He has to beg for the rest of his life?

"Let's play peek-a-boo or…"
She says quickly and afraid,
Trying to make him forget
Playing this one ever again.
He goes along with what she has said,

"ናብካ"

አብቲ መንገዳ ኦርብዓ
'ይሓይሽ' ኣብ ዝበለቶ ተጸጊዓ
ዝፍቀዳ ሳናቲም ኣብ ቅድሚኣ
ዝርካቡ ጉልባባ ንወዳ ኣማሚቓ
ድንን ምሽክንክን ሓዊሳ
ናብቲ ቀዘሒ ኢዳ ልኣኻ
ዕሽላ ክትዕንግል ስለ ዝነበራ
ከይፈተወት ከምኡ ጌራ
ጌና ብሓራሳ'ያ ሓጋዚ ስኢና
ዝርንዛሕ ነቢዓ ዕድላ ኣማሪራ
"ሓራስ ጓል ማርያም" ዘበላ
እነሆ ሕጂስ ዓሽኹላ
የጸውታ ኣሎ የዕልላ
"ማማየ'ቲ ጅንሒ ከልኤኪ"
"እንታይ?"
"ከምጁ"
ዝጸምለው ገጽ ተስፋ ተቖልቂሉ
ጸውቲ ሪኣ ስሒቓ ክትክውሓ

አብ ተጠንቀቕ ኢያ ኔራ
ተዋዲዱ ፍቅሪ
ንሱ ኸአ ከም ናታ ስለ ዝኸኣለ
ፍንጭሕጭሕ እናበለ
"ሸለ ማልያም?!" ኢልዋ ኢዱ እናሰደደ
ስንባደ ከም ሕሱም ዘበጣ
ኝኺይስበሎ ኣንፈጥሪጣ
ምስ ተበራበረት ካብቲ ዘኽንደዳ
ጌለ ነገር ክትገብር ተገዲዳ
ጀመረት ድማ ክትዝዝሮ
ነቲ ጸውቲ ቀደማ ነቲ ትዝክሮ
ኛው ኛው ኣቀናጥዋ ድሙ
                    ቲኽ ቲኽ
በዚኣ ጸጸ በዚኣ መላጸ
           እምባሕ
"ቱፍ እሞ በለለይ"

But one day he starts crying.
She says, "Let me kiss where it hurts,"
Hoping to soothe the pain
But then he kisses her
And asks, "Who hurt us?
Who should I hit?"
And demanding the name.
"Your father." She lets it slip.
Realizing what she has done,
She keeps quiet
Thinking she can still save her son.

"ቴፍ እሞ በልለይ"
ለመድዋ እቲ ሰሓቕ
ለመዶም ለመድዋ ምጽዋት

ሓደ መዓልቲ ግን
አይከምቀደሙን
ቀጨውጨው እብዚሑ
       ግና አይጠዓሞን
ሸዉ ምስ ተአበደ ብ "ቴፍ እሞ በለለይ"
ንሱ ድማ በለ "ቴፍ እሞ በልለይ
ንመን ቴፍ ክብለልኪ ማማየ"
"ነቦኻ!" በለቶ ሞሊቋዋ
አፉ ግን ዓበሰት ነታ ቓል
ትመልሳ መሲሉዋ።

Beyene Hailemariam

Silas

Silence so deep
It can be heard,
And a full moon –
A peaceful night,

Until a bird
Starts whispering,
Chirp, chirp, chirp.
He wants his mate

And over there
Right away
Another bird
Loud and clear

Replies, *I'm here*
For you, my hero.
Silas, listen.
Please don't be dense.

What the bird says
Is *yes* to love.
Silas, say *yes.*
Love's calling you.

Enough silence.
Answer *yes.*
If you give, you get,
And then we rock.
Silas, listen.
Please don't be dense.

ስላስ ሃንዛ ልባ

ለይቲ አጽቂጣ
ወርሒ አፍጢጣ፣
ወይ'ክ ዘዘው
እንትርርፊ ጸው.............!!

ሸዑ ግና............
ሓደ ዑፍ ቃዛኒ
ጨቕ ኢሉ ብወኒ.
ከይሰምዑ እንዳማጡ
ከድሂ አማኒቱ

ካብኡ ስግር ኢላ...
ካልእ ዑፍ ቆዛሚት
ጨቕ ተጸናጺነት፣
"አሎኹ.....ይኦኽሎ"
ኢላቶ ብቶሎ

ትሰምዒ'ዶ አሎኺ......???
ስላስ ሃንዛ ልባ
ግደፊ ስምዒ'ባ
ከምዛ ናይ ዑፍ ዋሪ
"ሆይ" በሊ ንፍቅሪ!!

ስላስ ሃንዛ ልባ
ልመዲ እንካ ሃባ
ከም ዕንዳይ ከም ሕንጢት
ካን ክብለኪ ባባ
ስላስ ሃንዛ ልባ...!!

40

Let's Divorce and Get Married Again

I worried about you
Having your first child,
But rising like the star
The wise men saw
You overcame my fear
And I bowed to your light.

It felt like an earthquake
As thunder filled the sky
And the seas seemed to part.
My world went wild,
Making my poetry soar
In the ululation
Of your opening life's door.

Not long after the birth
And christening, did someone make
You change, threatening
And pushing me away?
Could anyone give you more
Of his heart than me,
And giving it all for your sake?

So now what can I say?
If I whispered
In your ear, "Let's divorce
And get married again,"

ፈቲሐ'ዶ ክምርዓወኪ?

በኳር ብምንባርኪ
ብዙሕ ፈሪሀልኪ፣
ግን.....ዘይከምዝፈራሁኹዎ
.....ከምተመኘኹዎ፣
ኮኾብኪ ተራእዩ
ቀደድ ኢሉ ወለል፣
ሰጊዶ ኣብ ብርሃንኪ
ኮይነ ሰብኣ-ሰገል።

ዕላልን ዕልልታን
ድርሳን ኩዳን ስብራን
መሬት ኣሕመድሚዱ፣
ብላዕሊ ነጕዱ
ባሕሪ ኣንበድቢዱ፣
ባብኪ ተኾፈቲ
ገዓት ተጋዒቲ።

ዋእ.....ግና..........
ልደትን ጥምቀትን
ዓመትን መንፈቕን
ኣሕልፍ ምስ'በልክስ
ትሓናፍጥኒ??!!
ተወጣውጥለይ??!!

ኣቋሚትኪ ዘሕሰለዉ
ረሲዐክዮ ዝሓለዉ?
በሊ እስከ'ባ.......
ከመይ....ስለምንታይ
ኣለኪ ድዩ ኸማይ
ገሚዑ ዝበኪ ልቡ ኣብ ውንጭሕቲ
ሂቡ ሂብ ዘይብል...ዘይኮነ ሕፍንቲ!!

ስለ.....ስለ.....ሕጂ ግና
ናይ ብኡነት ብቕንዕና

42

Would you feel better,
Like you did back then?

አብ ጕንዲ እዝግኺ ሕሹኽ'የ ክብለኪ
"ቀሩብ ተሓሸኪ
ፈቲሐ'ዶ ክምርዓወኪ?"

For Twenty Nakfa

An old friend of mine,
A big bore and a wild liar
With long hair like a monk,
Asked me for twenty nakfa.

Was I stupid to say yes?
What's twenty nakfa?
It's a small price to pay.
God bless him, now he stays away.

ሳላ ዕስራ ቅርሺ

ሓደ መተዓብይተይ.............
          ተርሲሳ ዘኣሙሉ
          ኪሕ ዝብል ዕላሉ
          ዝጋፍያ ፈላሲ
          ዝሕሱ ብዕሲ
          አለቂሐዮ'ሲ
          ሓድ- ቀኑብ ሰላዲ.............
.........ክልተ ዓመቱ ካብ ዘይርእዮ አብ ዓዲ

          ሳላ ዕስራ ቅርሺ
          ሸይጠሉ ስክፍታ
          (ገዚኣ) ግን ሩፍታ
          ሰኣን ቀኑብ ቅርሺ
          ክትነብሪ'ዶ ኮንኪ
          ነብሰይ ክትቅሸሺ?!

Fessehaye Yohannes

If He Came Back

If he came back to life in our harsh land
Even in disguise and for a moment,
We would recognize a precious pearl
And protect it from the roadside thieves.

We would see a stately tree providing
Shade but needing to be protected
Itself from the grueling sun to survive,
And we would offer our purest water.

But nobody can change the fact he's dead
Or question it. He won't come back again.

He rode the razor's edge for twenty years.
His feet never touched the ground, only thorns.
Every torch he passed burned with his hope,
But he didn't see it end in victory
As we do now that the haze and darkness
Burn away revealing unobstructed
And smooth highway where we stand in mourning,
Silenced by our fallen hero except
To say our faith endures to honor him

And we still need to see him back with us
However briefly in this brutal place
Of too many heroes and martyrs yet
With him shining forth and solid: the pillar
At the center of our vision, struggle
And pain to make our nation – passion

"ሓንሳብ 'ተዝቅልቀል"

ሓንሳብ 'ተዝቅልቀል ናብ'ዛ ከዳዕ መሬት
ዋላ ፃዕልኢት ከኾይኑ ፋሉይ ፍጥረት፣
ምሓየብናዮ ከም'ዛ ሉል ናይ ባሕሪ
ከይዘዎምቶ ከይከትሮ ዘራፊ ሽታሪ።

ከም ምዕርግቲ ተኽሊ ስዊት ናይ ገደና
እምብዛ 'ንበቃ ጸሓይ ከይኾና
ከይትቅምስል ኢልና ምሒር ንከናኸና
ስጋብ'ቲ ዓቅምን ከበንበን ምበልና።

አበይ'ሞ ንባህርይ መን ይገጥሞ
ገባሪት ሓዳጊት ዘይብላ ዳኛ።

ዋግዋጎ ምስ ኮነ ጸላም ምስ ተገፈ
ሕልኸልኸ ተሰጊሩ ጽርጎያ ምስ ጸፈፈ፣
20 ዓመቱ አብ በሊሕ መላጸ
አሻኹ ሰጊሩ ለምለም ከይረገጸ፣
ፋና ወሊዑ ተስፋ ምስ አስነቐ
ኡፍ! እንከይበለ ጅግና 'ንተወደቐ፣
መሬት ጸልሚቱ ሕርብት'ዩ ዝብለካ
መትከል ግን ሓያል'ዩ ሞቱ የኾርናካ።

ሓንሳብ 'ተዝቅልቀል ናብ'ዛ ከዳዕ መሬት
እቲ ጅግና ጃጋኑ ሓደ ካብ ሰማእታት

ድልዱል ዓንዲ ማእከል ጸዋር ማእገር
ተጸዋራይ ሕሰም ተቓላሳይ አርሒ ሃገር
ናይ ትብዓት ናይ ርቀት ሓያል መምህር።

እታ ሽዉ ዘወደቐት ተታኺሲት
ከመይ ንቋሕ-ለም፣ እዎ! ፃዕልኢት
ዓቅሊ ጌራ እምቢ ዘይምበለት
ጅግና ካብ ትወስድ ጅግና ጐይታ መሬት!

Courage and powerful art — like him.

Seeing such a target, the fatal shot
Should have disobeyed the trigger's order
To end our son's and struggle's brightest day.

Instead it means his memory and name
And proudly moving on because of them,

Yet most proudly on the anniversary
Of his death, now a part of our history,
Making the soil we buried him within
Blessed and envied sheltering our hero
And bearing light that's sure to spread and reign
Throughout our land, although until that day,
When we will also build a worthy tomb
For his remains, we guard his rough stone grave
As the sanctuary of our best pearl

And we still need to see him back with us
However briefly in this brutal place
Of too many heroes and martyrs yet

Like gold to us, tested in the fire and
Made ever more beautiful and true by
His experience and through becoming
Our commitment, too: the cause we follow —
Resistance despite despair at his loss —

And the compass giving us direction
Because he knew what we all had to do

And did it first, this hero of heroes
Who volunteered to die before him but

እታ መመልከቲቾ'ታ ስሓቢት ቃታ
እስር ዘይምበለት ህላወ ስሒታ
ጅግና ካብ ትወስድ ዘይብሉ መስታ።።

ንዓይ ጸላም'ያ አብ ጉዕዞ ታሪኽና
እታ መዓልቲ'ቲኣ ዝወሰደት ጅግና፡
ክቡር ወላድ ነይሩ ሰውራና ዘፍረየቶ
እዛ ጸላም መዓልቲ ግን ንዓ ገይራ'ቶ።።

እንተ ንሳ'ሞ ኮረዓ
ብሸም ሓደ ጅግና ተጸዊዓ
አብ መዝገብ ሰፈራ
ክትዝከር ምንባራ።።

ዕድለኛ መሬት ንዕኡ ዝስተረት
ካብ ኩሉ ከባቢኣ ትከበር ትነየት።።
ስጋብ ምሉእ ብርሃን አብ ሃገር ዝሰፍን
ሓወልቲ ንተኸለላ ንገዝኩሩ ዝኾውን
ጨርሒ እምና ክንሕልም ኢና
ስታሪት ክቡር ዕንቀኑና ኢያ ስታሪት እቲ
ጅግና።።

ሓንሳብ 'ተዝቆልቀል ናብ'ዛ ክዳዕ መሬት
እቲ ጅግና ጀጋኑ ሓደ ካብ ሰማእታት

ወርቂ ከምዝፍተን ሓዊ ተለብሊቡ
መዋጥራት ሰጊሩ'ዩ ተመኮሮ ደሊቡ
ሓድጊ ኸአ ገዲፉ አሰሩ ዝስዕቡ፡
አጆኻ ቅስን አለናልካ ዝብሉ ብሸግር ዘይስነፉ
ክምህ ዘይብሉ ንሱ ብምሕላፉ።።

ቡሶላ እምበርዶ'ታ ሓባሪ ጉዕዞና
አንፈት ከይስሓተ ቅኑዕ ዝመርሓና!

ነዚ ኩሉ ጅግና አምሳያኡ ሕለፍ 'ተዝብልዎ
ኩሉ ምጉየየ ክስዋእ ተኪእዎ

Whom he wanted to save in the struggle.

More than other gems, diamonds create
Jealousy, but only for their beauty.

More than other plants, green grass seems fresh.
It fades and burns without enough water
And, as the prophet says, all flesh is grass,
But similarly denied, our hero thrived
Like a lion, the strongest animal,
Yet stronger, showing mercy and knowing
The difference between enemies and friends,

And we still need to see him back with us
However briefly in this brutal place
Of too many heroes and martyrs yet

Like…a pearl? A stately shade tree needing
Our protection? A pillar of light? Gold?
A compass? A diamond? The riches of
Grass or flesh? The mighty lion? Words
And comparisons cannot say enough
Of what we feel at the loss of our friend
And his embrace – its power quick as life
And great as change itself – with his mere glance
Frightening away our worst enemies.

He lived up to the heroes before him,
And died in the struggle – gone forever
Except in the ever-expanding fields
And the solid ground of our country's cause,

ንምንታይሲ ንጅግና እውን ጅግና'ለዎ።

ካብ ማዕድናት ኩሉ ዝበለጸት ነገር
አልግዝ ምሡረጽኩ 'ተማበለኒ ሃረሪ
እንተኾነ አልማዝ ካብ ጌጽ ሐሊፉ የብላን
ቁም-ነገር።

ካብ አቑጽልቲ ኩለን አዝያ ተባሃጊት
ስየ ምመረጽኩ ናይ ዓይነይ መዐረፊት
እንተኾነ ስየ ትቕምስል ትሐርር
ማይ እንተስኢና ትነቕጽ ቶኹምተር
ንሱ ግን ጸዋርዮ ዋላ ነቲ ምድረ ሃሩር።

ካብ እንስሳ ኩሎም ሐይል ምመረጽኩ
አንበሳ ምበልኩ ዓይነይ ከይሐሰኹ።
አንበሳ ግን ንኾኩ ሐደዩ ጨካን ባሩ
ፈታዊ ጸላኢ ዘይፈሊ ንሕስያ ዘይብሉ።

ሐንሳብ 'ተዝቅልቀል ናብ'ዛ ከዳዕ መሬት
እቲ ጅግና ጀጋኑ ሐደ ካብ ሰማእታት
ስምየ ስኢነሉ ብኽብሪ ርእየዮ
ልዕሊ ኹሉ ነገር ላዕሊ ሰቒለዮ፣
አልማዝ፣ ስየ ኢለ ሸም ከይጥምቐ
አየዕግቡንንዮም ማዕሪ'ቲ ዘድንቐ።

ከይሸሞ አንበሳ፣ 'ቲ ሐይል እንስሳ
ተዓጻጸፈ'ዩ ባህሩ፣ መማዱ ሐንጎሉ።

ገጹ እስር የብል ክርኢ ጸላእቱ
ፍትሕ የብሎ አብ ቅድሚ ፈተውቱ።

ጅግና ከምቶም ዝቐደሙ
ሂወቱ ዘሕለፈ ታሪኹ ብወርቂ አቐሊሙ።

ንሱ ተኸዊሉ ጽላሉ ግን አሎ
ዓብዩ ዘጉላዕልዕ ሜዳ ዘይአኽሎ
ሱር ዝሰደደ ማንም ዘይብንቁሮ።

52

Where we stay rooted, kept from following
Him now though continuing in his stride
Before we go forever to his side.

አክንድኡ ኮይነ አብ ቦትኡ 'ተዘይአተኹ
ብሕጊ ናይ ባህሪ ስለዝተቋየድኩ
ማሕላ ይቕሥነኒ አሰሩ ክሰዕብ
ብኽብሪ ክምዝገብ አብ'ቲ ናቱ መዝገብ።

Reesom Haile

Voice

Speech online
Can set you free
It lights my voice
On a screen like the sun

Voice. Voice!
The net sets me free
To think in poetry
The sad will rejoice
The weeping will laugh

In the news like food and drink
In the dark with a candle to think

Sisters, brothers, citizens, drums!
ezm! z-ezm! ezm! z-ezm!
ebum! b-ebum! ebum! b-ebum!
Voice! Voice!

We share the screen
Like the sun
And our freedom of speech
Reads the poetry in thought

ደሃይ

ደሃየ! ደሃየ!
እንኪ ሓሳበይ
ስጥሕለይ አብ ጸሓየ።
ደሃየ! ደሃየ!
አጸናንዕለይ ዝጕሃየ
አብድለይ ዝበኸየ
ዓንግልለይ ዝጠመየ
አስትይለይ ዝጸምአየ
ሰላም በልለይ
ንደቂ ዓደየ
ደሃየ! ደሃየ!
አብርህለይ ላምባየ
መሬት ምስ መሰየ
እስኪ ኸበር
እ-ዝም! ዝ-እዝም! እ-ዝም! ዝ-እዝም!
እ-ቡም! ብ-እቡም! እ-ቡም! ብ-እቡም!
ደሃየ
እንኪ ሓሳበይ
ስጥሕለይ አብ ጸሓየ
እንኪ ሓሳበይ
ስጥሕለይ አብ ጸሓየ።።

We Have

We have men and women
Who sacrifice their lives.
We have a nation.
We have women and men
To gather and provide.
Men and women who lead.
We have independence.
We have equality and justice
We have women and men.
We have black, white, and red.
We have men and women
Without end in the struggle
To grow, study and persist.
Who think and think again
To teach, learn and know.
We have women and men
Without the lust for power.
Who stand up or down
With our consent.
We have God and a future.
We have men and women
Who belong in our nation
And we belong with them.
Rejoice, I say it again.
We have women and men.
Rejoice.

አለዉና / አለዋና

ንሃገሮም/ንሃገረን ህይወቶም/ህይወተን
ዘሕለፉ/ዘሕለፉ
ንሃገሮም/ንሃገረን ናጽነት ዘትረፉ/ዘትረፉ
ንሀዝቦም/ንሀዝበን ዝመርሑ/ዝመርሓ
ዝጥርንፉ/ዝጥርንፉ
አለዉና/አለዋና
ንፍትሕን ንፍርድን ዘወናጨፉ/ዘወናጨፉ
ሌላን ጉሌላን ዝጽይፉ/ዝጽይፉ
ዘይብሉና/ዘይብላና ቀይሑ/ቀይሓ
ሓርፈፉ/ሓርፈፉ
አለዉና/አለዋና
ንሃገር ከማዕብሉ/ከማዕብላ ዝጻደፉ/ዝጻደፉ
ንመጻኢና ዝሓስቡ/ዝሓስባ
ዝፈላስፉ/ዝፈላስፉ
ዝምህሩ/ዝምህራ ዝመሃሩ/ዝመሃራ
ዘንብቡ/ዘንብባ ዝጽሕፉ/ዝጽሕፉ
አለዉና/አለዋና
ብፍቓድና ዝስለፉ/ዝስለፉ
ብፍቓድና ዝግለፉ/ዝግለፉ
ንስልጣን ዘይሃርፉ/ዘይሃርፉ
አለዉና/አለዋና፡፡
ናይ እግዚኄር ንግዚኄር
ናይ ብሔር ንብሔር
ዝገድፉ/ዝገድፉ
አለዉና/አለዋና
ክሓልፈልና እንድዩ ክሓልፈልና፡፡

58

Ghirmai Ghebremeskel

A Candle for the Darkness

Fight for freedom?
You want to fight for freedom
Because you love this country
And live to see it free
And overflowing with promise?
You only want to drink freedom,
Whatever it takes?

Accept this candle and go.
It is freedom and its promise,

All you need to see,
The only light
And enough to keep you warm

When every day
Is nothing but death
And more death,
Hunger and more hunger,
War and more war,

And you add to it,
Because you're strong
And know what it takes,
Sacrificing yourself,
Like the candle with its light,
Standing straight and tall.

But even warmed to the heart

ቀንዴል ጸልማት

ተዋጋኢ፤
ብሕጂ ዚጥጋእ፤
ድጉን ሓርበኛ፤
ንናጽነትን ብተስፋአን ዚነብር፤

ብኣአ ዚዕንገል፤
ንዓአ ዚውፊ፤

ጉዕዞአ ብሓንቲ ቀንዴል ይበርህ፤
ናይ ተስፋ ቀንዴል
ናይ ናጽነት ቀንዴል፤

ናብ'ቲ ዘብርሃቶ ደረት ትርኢት ይስሓብ፤
ብብርሃና ይበርሆ፤
ብምጆታ ይመጆ ፨

ኣብ ሕማቕ ግዜ፤
ጭንቂ ምስ በዝሐ፤
ሞት ምስ በዝሐ፤

ሞት ብጥሜት፤
ሞት ብኹናት፤
ኢሰብኣዊ ሞት፤

ንግዳይ ናይ'ዚ ዕንወት
መንፈሳዊ ሓይሉ
ኡንኮ ኣለንታኡ

ዘይትጠፍእ፤ ዘይትሃስስ ቀንዴል ጸላም
ትርኣዮ ኣብ ዓይኒ ሓንጎሉ፤

ሙቐት ትውልዕ ኣብ ልቡ፤
ብኹርዓት ተጎንያ ንክሳዱ፤

You'll still ask, why
The murder
And mutilation
Of children
And anything alive?

What is a world
With no birdsong,
And no fragrant flowers
To attract the bees?

Will there come a time
When we're not haunted
By devils and death
In the shadows,
Even scaring the angels?

Believe me, I see
Days when the horror
Will end, and the birds
Will sing again;

When the bees
Will dance out of the blossoms
With their honey,
And life itself will breathe,
Normal again.

I see these days
When the horror will end,
And our future like a candle
Comes out of the darkness
And lights up the horizon

እንታይ ግዜኡ’ዮ’ዚ?
ግዜ ጮጅ ማጮጅ፣
ጸረ-ሀጸን ዝጭከነሉ፣
ዕሸላት ዚሰንክለሉ፣
ህይወት ዝሕረሙሉ፣

እንታይ ግዜኡ’ዮ’ዚ?
አዕዋፍ ዘይዝምራሉ፣
ዕምባባ ዘይሸተተሉ፣
ንህቢ ዘይዝምብየሉ፣

እንታይ ግዜኡ’ዮ’ዚ?
ግዜ ጮጅ ማጮጅ፣ ግዜ ጎሓሉ፣
መልኣኽ ሞት ዝኾርዓሉ፣
መልኣኽ ህይወት ዝደነሉ።
አብ ዓይኒ ሕልናይ፣
ይርአየኒ አሎ፣
ግዝኣት ጮጅ ማጮጅ ከኸተም እንከሎ።
ይርአየኒ ኩሉ፣-
አዕዋፍ መዝሙረን ኬስምዓ፣

ዕምባባታት ሕብርታቶም ኪድርጉሑ፣
ንህቢ ኪመላለስ፣ ኪተግህ፣-
ኬምዕር፣
ትንፋስ ኪዘርእ፣
ህይወት ናብ ግቡእ ዓንከላ
ክትመጽእ።

ግዝኣት ጮጅ ማጮጅ ከኸተም ከሎ፣
አብ ዓይኒ ሕልናይ ይርአየኒ አሎ።
ቀንዴል ጸልማት ንመጻኢ፣ ከተብርሆ፣
ደረት ትርኢት ክትውልዖ፣
ይርአየኒ ብዓይኒ አእምሮ።

ብዙሓት ሰባት ይርአዩኒ፣-
ናብቲ ብርሃን ኪኸዱ፣
ነቲ ብርሃን ኪዓጉ፣

62

Brimming with people
Marching into the light –
Candles and more candles
Coming from all directions,
Giving each other their flame
And joining together in one hall.

I see them all refusing
Any more death,
And restoring, adoring
And rejoicing in life.

ካብ'ቲ ብርሃን ኪካፈሉ፣
        እዳሞም ኪህቡ፣
                እዳሞም ኪወስዱ።

ብዙሓት ሰባት ይርአዩኒ፣-
        ካብ ኩሉ ኩርናዕ ኪመጹ፣
                ናብ'ቲ አዳራሽ ኪአትዉ፣
                        ኪተአኻኸቡ።

ኩሎም ይርአዩኒ፣-
        ኪሃንጹ፣
                ኪጸግቡ፣
                        ኪስሕቁ፣

                        ኪነብሩ - ንሞት
                        ኪብድሁ፣
                        ንህይወት ኬምልኹ።

64

ዕረቛና

ዕረቛና ግዳ ምስቲ ሕንግድ
ዝኣበየ ምጽዓድ
ዘይሕብረይ ወሪሱ
ጸልማት እናቚብአ

ክፍንጥስ ደልዩ ገግናዩ እናጋብአ
ተሸ.....ኸ ተባሂልና
ተራሓሒ ቛና ኬንና ሕቛን ክብድን
ከይንባተኽ ከአ ገያሽን መገድን

አይ አብ ሜዳ አይ አብ ሩባ
አይ ብባሩድ አይ ብኻራ
ገጢምናልኩም ቅልስ
መን ጐብለል ዘይምለስ
ንሱ አለዎ መረዋሕ
ስዉር ዓሊ.ወሊ.ውታ
አነ ኝኸይዓርፍ

ዝገማድሕ ዝጀላልሕ
ተኻሲስና ምስ ነበሰይ
አይ ብርስቲ አይ ብጕልቲ
ዕረቛና ግዳ
ክኾነኩም ንጽድቒ

ወይስ ከሕልፍ እዚ ዕረተይ
እዋን አብ ቅልስ
ሓደው ክጽሊ ጨሪሱ
ክብንጠስ
እምበር ክሳብ መዓስ ድአ
ክሕመስ።

Fortuna Ghebreghiorgis

Help Us Agree

When will my shadow
And I agree?
Why won't it obey?
Whenever I wear colors
Darkness comes back at me.

We live in a tug of war.
Normal slips into weird.
Back or stomach,
Traveler or road,
Field or river —

We're never separate,
But we have opposing views,
And fight like gun and knife
Until neither wins
And I can't get any rest,

Always tied to darkness
And hearing the waves and shore
As if they accuse each other.
Should I pray for my shadow and me
To try to agree

Or simply continue
This blind, sad battle
In the hope
That I will be redeemed
Before I fade away?

Solomon Drar

Who Said Merhawi Is Dead?

Buried in the ground
Heaped with stones,
Silent and at peace,
Merhawi comes home,
Back to his land –
Desert, highlands
And fields he farmed.
Is Merhawi dead?

His mother stands proud
And his bed blossoms.
From near and far
His sisters and brothers
Come and sing
"Thanks, Merhawi, thanks,"
As they stroll down
Liberation Avenue.

"We love Merhawi!
Yeah Merhawi!"
Who said Merhawi is dead
And rots in a grave,
Or that the Red Sea salt
Eats him, and the frost
North on Rora
Burns his skin,

If we see his blood
Shimmering in our veins,
Stride with him

መርሃዊ ሞይቱ ዝብልዎ
መኣስ ሞይቱ!

ካብ መሬቱ፣ ኣብ መሬቱ፣ ናብ መሬቱ፣
ኣብ ምድረበዳ ጎልጎል፣
ኣብ ኣኽራናት ገደል፣
ብሓመድ - እምኒ ተጸፊጡ፣
ዋላ የጽትጥ ብድቃስ ተዋሒጡ፣
መኣስ'ሞ ሞይቱ መርሃዊ!

ዝወለደቶ ማህጸን ኮሪዓ፣
ዝደቀሰሳ መሬት ጠቢዓ፣
ዝናፍቕዎ ኣሓት ኣሕዋት፣
መላእ ሕብረተ-ሰብ ቀረባ ርሑቓት፣
ሳልኡ! ሳልኡ! ሳልኡ! እናበሉ
ኣብ ጕደና ሓርነት ሸኖዕ ኪብሉ፣
ንሱ ደ'ይኮነን ህያውነት መርሃዊ!!

ኣይመሽመሽን!

ጨው ሰሊና ኣይበልያን ኣዕጽምቱ፣
ኣይመጠጉን!
ቀዝሒ ሮራ ኣይጨምደደን ቆርበቱ፣
ምስጠሉ ኢዩ ዘሎ ደሙ፣
ናብ መትንታትና ልሒሙ፣
እነሀና'ንዶ ንወሳወስ፣
እንተዝመውት ድኣ ዘይንልኹሰስ?
እነሀና'ንዶ ንርኢ ንስተውዕል፣
እንተዝመውት ድኣ ዘይንዓውር?
መርሃዊ ሞይቱ ዝብል ድኣ መን'ዩ?
ካብ ንፋስ ሓርነት ዘየዳምጽ ድሃዩ።

ርግጽ!
በብራኹ እንተዘይኬድና፣

Instead of limping,
And see for miles
Instead of being blind?

Who said Merhawi is dead?
Can't they hear
Merhawi, Merhawi,
In the whirlwind
Of the revolution?
We must walk with his knees,
See with his eyes
And live by his words
Or we fall like unripe fruit
Into corruption,

Selfishness and greed,
And the rot spreads
With no respect
Or care until
Oblivion cracks
Us limb by limb,
Enemies pour in
From all directions

And the answer to
"Is Merhawi dead"
Will be "Yes. It's true,"
Meaning our end, too,
Instead of his vision
For our future:
Working together
Like water and milk

And a perfect fit

በዒንቱ እንተዘይተመሪሕና፡
ቃሉ ብዘይምኽባር፡
ብጉዑ እንተወዲቑ ፍረና፡
ብሀርፋኑ ስልጣን
ብኣድልዎ ወገን
ረሲኣን ኩይና ምስእንነዳዳኽ፡
ንጸላእቲ ምስእንፈጥር ፈቓቅ፡
ሞተ ማለት ሽዉ መርሃዊ፡
ብኣርባዕተ መአዝን የእዊ።

እንተዘየለ፡
ከም ማይን ጸባን፡
ከም ኢድን ማንካን፡
ተዋሃሂድና፡
ዋልታ ሓድነት ገቲርና፡
ቃሉ ምስዘይነዕብር፡
ሳሾያ እንተኢልና ንህንጸት ሃገር፡
ሎሚ ኣይሞተ፡ ጽባሕ ኣይመውት መርሃዊ፡
ህያውዩ ዘለኣለማዊ።

ናይ ሚልዮናት ኣዒንቲ፡
ናይ ኣዳራሽ መብራህቲ፡
ሓዘን ኣይድልዮን ብኺያት፡
ተስካር ኣየድልዮን ፍትሓት፡
ህያውዩ በዓል ፋረ'ምበሳ፡
ጻድቅ'ዩ ዘይብሉ ኣበሳ።

መርሃዊ ሞይቱ ዝብል መን'ዩ?
ካብ ንፋስ ሓርነት ዘየዳምጽ ድሃዩ፡

70

Of hand and glove –
Eager for the test
To build our nation
Today, tomorrow
And always with him
Who will never die
Showing the way:

One glorious beam
And millions of eyes
Knowing how to shine
With no need for tears
And memorials . . .
But only if Merhawi lives!
Only if the lion slayer
Lives unrepentantly,

His name, *Merhawi, Merhawi*
In the whirlwind
Of the revolution!
Can you hear?
Who said Merhawi is dead?
Can they save us
Like his name,
Harvesting the fields of gold?
Who said Merhawi is dead?

መርሃዊ ጥይቱ ዝብል ተጋዋዩ፣
ብወርቃዊ ምህርቱ ወርትግ ህያውዩ።

Ghirmai Yohannes (San Diego)

Like a Sheep

Led with a rope around his neck,
He blindly followed the trader
And the butcher and blithely thought
Of grazing in a new country.

They gave him their official seal
And off he went, but they forgot
Or lost his documentation,
Which he never bothered to get.

Now he is stuck. What will he do?
Are they his biggest problem?
Back home he's forgotten.
He forgets where he is, too.

በጊዕ

በጊዕ ኣእምሮ የብሉን ብኡኑት
ክሕረድ ጐቲቶም እናወስድዋ ብገመድ
ን "ወጻኢ" እየ ገኸይድ ዘለኹ
ኢሉ ስለ ዝሓሰበ
ደድሕሪቶም ነጋዲ......ዦኸዦ እናበለ ሰዓበ
ሻቡ ሓደ ሓራዲ ሓደ ነጋዲ
ቪዛ ወቒያምሉ ብወግዒ
ኣብ ምንታዩ ከም ዝወቐዕሉ
እግዚኤር ዋንኡም እንድዒ
ብድሕሪኡ በታ ቪዛኡ
ንወጻኢ ምስ ሰገሩ
በጊዕ ደሃዮም ኣይገበረ
ንሳቶም ደሃዩ ኣይገበሩ።።

Unjust Praise

In the beginning
The spirit moving
Upon the face of the waters
And in the breaking waves
Tasted salt

And I see fields of it
Drying on the shore.
We let in shallow lakes of sea
To evaporate,
And the salt

Accumulates along their edge
Thanks to the sunlight:
Crystal white,
Enough for everyone,
Harvested and sold

In every shop and on the roads:
Salt! —
In proper measure
Bringing out the taste,
The flavor and spirit

Of our food, hot or cold.
Why should pepper get
So much admiration
When salt does all the work?

ከንቱ ውዳሴ

ካብ መፋጥርቱ -
መናብርቱ ተሰሊዑ -
ካብ ማይ ባዳ፣ ማይ ባሕሪ ተጨንጒዑ።

እብ ግርሁ ጨው ተገቢቱ -
ንብርሃን ቀትሪ ተሰጢሑ
መማዩ ተመምዩ ሃፊፉ -
ብጸሓይ ቆላታት ተጸንፊፉ።

ንሱ ጨው ኩይኑ -
ይተርፍ እብ ምድሪ -
ቶኸሚሩ ተሓፊሱ ንከገልግል መመቀሪ።

እብ ዕዳጋ ይስራዕ -
ብ"ኮንትሮባንዳ" ዘይኩነስ ብዕሊ -
በብመአዝኑ ይዋፈር በብመቑነኑ ብስፍሪ።

እናሓንሳብ ብጥርኡ
ወይ'ውን ተደቚሱ -
ጥዑም ጣዕሚ እናሃበ አብ ብልዕና ተነስኒሱ።

እብ ውዑይን ዝሓሙልን ሓቒቑ -
ተመጢኑ ተዳዊሱ ምስ ቀመማት ተሓሚሱ -
ቃና መቀረት ዝምጡ ርእሲ ኹሎም ክነሱ -
እንታይ'ቲ ምኽንያቱ?
ውሽጡና ንዳህሰስ -
ጨው ዘመቀረልና በርበረ ንውድስ!!

76

Next Time Ask

One fact won't go away.
Tomorrow or today
You have to know you die.
Don't think of asking why.

Your pain should leave no doubt.
In no time you'll be out.

The hole you never saw,
The crash you don't expect,
The condition no one detects.
They're the law.

Full of trust and working hard,
You taste success,
Triumph – the crowd roars "yes!"
And dust is your reward.

At your reincarnation
Why not raise your voice.
"I've been human before.
Is it the only choice?

Why must I always weep?
Can I come back as a sheep,
A monkey or a boar
To fall through the trap door?"

ኣማኽሩኒ

ሎሚ ወይ ጽባሕ-
ሞት ንዘይቐሪ፣
ናብራ ዓለም ጭንቀት
ዘንተእለት ወጥሪ።
ኣብ ነብሲ ወከፍ ስጉምቲ - ካብኡ ናብኣ ስድሪ
መሰናኽል ኣሎ - ዕንቅፋት ናይ
ባህሪ-ተደጐለ ጓህሪ

ንዓኣ ኣሚኑ - ወዲ ኣዳም ኣማኒ
ነዛ ተበጣሲት - ተበታኺት ፈትሊ
ይሃልኽ ወትሩ ይጽዕር -
ክሳብ ዘሎ ኣብ ምድሪ!
መዋእሉ ከየዕረፈ ብሞቱ ይበሪ፣
ጠንቂ'ዚ ትዕድልታቱ "ሰብ"፣ "ሰብ" ምዃኑ'ዩ
ሰሪ!!
ስለዚ......ምስ'ሞትኩ ኣብ ምላሽይ
ምናልባት!! ምረጽ'ተበለኒ ፈጣሪ፣
እስከ ኣማኽሩኒ
መፍለስ'ዶ ክኸውን በጊዕ ይሕሸኒ?

Who Needs a Story?

I needed a story
And asked myself all day –
What can I write?
It kept me awake all night –
What do I have to say?

I emptied so many words
And ideas out of my brain
It would have floated away
If not tied to my heart.
Now I needed art.

Paper and pen in hand,
Tomorrow I would start . . .
But wait.
What is this all about?
Do I really need a story?

All this time and hard work –
For what?
I hate myself for thinking this.
I already have a story
That nobody knows and it's great –
I am the story.

ጽውጽዋይ ጽሓፊ

መዓልትን ለይትን ደኺመ
ረርካ ዘይድቅስ ጸር ሓሳባት ሓዚለ
ተጨኒቐ! ውሻጠ ኣእምሮይ ሓሊበ፡
ሓሳብ ንሓሳብ ኣጋጭየ - ቃላት ኣብ ሽክናይ ሓቑነ፡
ዘዝጽዓየለይ መሪጸ ብልበይ ዛንታ ቀዊደ፡
ብርዐይ ወረቐተይ ኣዋሃሂደ-ተ-ዋ-ዲ-ደ፡
ትማሊ ምሸት ተኣንቲተ - ጽውጽዋይ ክጽሕፍ ሃቀነ።

    ግን'ከ ከንቱ'ዩ ነይሩ ዘየድሊ ድኻም፡
    ግዜካን ሓንጎልካን "ንብላሽ" ምብኻን፡
    ከመይሲ!...............
    ጽውጽዋይ ምጽሓፍ ኣይመድለየንን ንዓይ፡
    ዋላ ኣይፈለጥ ምዕራፍ መወዳእታይ፡
    እናኹ'ንዶ ባዕለይ ጽብቕቲ ጽውጽዋይ።
        ኽላ ሎምስ ንዲቓ'ያ - መዚነያ ነብሰይ፡
        ጽውጽዋይ ከሰኹስ - ጽውጽዋይ ምጽሓፈይ።

80

Paulos Netabay

Remembering Sahel

Who could forget the war?
The battles where we fell,
The awful sun, our wounds
Glistening like jewels
In the hell we've never left . . .

Yet more: always barefoot,
Always thorns, refusing
To go on except
For one more step, deeper
Into Sahel . . . remember?

Give me your hands to write
The names again now
And for tomorrow's sake –
Baquos, Ela-babu,
Itaro – places still bright

As the tears in our eyes
Recalling how good
And welcome we felt there:
Amberbeb, Halibet,
Hishkib, Himbol, Hager

And Arerb . . . remember
Mountain after mountain,
Armies of ghostly killers
On all night marches?
Sahel, I march again.

ንዝክር

ንዝክር ዎ ጸርና ለመሪር ኣውካድ ንዳል
ርሳስ ዐላ ሰርነና ትከክ ኢኮን ወተላል
ክብድ እባ ኦፋሃ
ጸሓይ ምስል ተውነታ
ትፈንቴናሃ ክል ሰኔት እግል ትትመም ሽንሀታ።
                ተጋይ ዐላ እገርና ዎ ካየድናሁ ለኣሸዋክ
                ምርወት "ኒጊስ" ትብል ዎ "ኣቤኮ"
                ልብል ኣብሪክ
                ፋሕ፡ መንተብሊ ዎ ዔላዕር
                ባቆስ፡ ዔላባቡ ዎ ዒታሮ
                ተእሪክ እግል ልትከተብ፡ ክማ ህዳይ
                ትፈረሮ።
ሰፋለልኮ ዎውላድ ህጀክ ወለሕዋሊ
እት ገጽ-ገጯ ትጋየሳ፡ መስከብ ሓዮት ልትፈሊ
ሃገር፡ ህምቦል ዎ ዓሬርብ
ዓምበርበብ፡ ሓሊበት ዎ ሕሸክብ
እገር ዐላ ልትቃሲ ዎ ዐንታት ቤላ "ይእሰክብ"።
                ፈገርናሁ ለኣድብር፡ ላሊ ጊስና ዎ ኣምዕል
                ትካረፍናሁ ኣባይና፡ ሮራ እምቤ ዎ ስሕል
                ዓጋመት፡ እንሲ ዎ ኣምባ
                ሓልሓል፡ ኣሪግ ዎ ናቅፋ
                ኢንትረሳዕ ዎ ሓወዬ ንዳግሞ ለሓልፉ።
ሕቃብ ኢኮን ዎ ክባብ፡ ጽዋር ዐላ እት መርከብ
ሕና ዐላና እናድል፡ ኣስክ ረሀዮት ትትረከብ
ሮራ ሓባብ ዎ ኣስራይ
መርሳ ግልቡብ ዎ ታክላይ

82

Rora, I don't forget.
Amba, Insi, Agamet,
Your trenches in my head.
Hal-hal, Arag, Nakfa,
You buried our dead.

We hear them in your names,
The struggle and the war
We carried on our backs,
Unsure of the end,
Except it led to your door.

Rora-habab, Asray,
Forts, say what you know.
Marsa-gulbub, Marsa-teklay,
Harbors, testify
To the brutality

We suffered to breathe freedom
Finally on May 24.
A chorus joined our war:
Ayget, Qatar, Denden,
Ashorm, Tikse, Koken —

Rough song in a rough land
Where lions also lived.
But it delivered
Our enemies to our hands,
Protected our children,

Wrote what we did in blood
And offered rocks, caves and trees
Where we hid in the shade

ከሀልናሃ ለመራር፡ አስክ ጅምዐት ለአምዕላይ።
ለሀይ ምን ለሀይ ኢሐምቅ፡ ወደግ
ልግባእ ወደብር
ሕጌ ገብእ እግልና ዎ አባይ ሀላ
ለትጋዕር
ዐይገት፡ ቀጣር ዎ ደንደን
ዓሸርም፡ ትክሴ ዎ ኮከን
እብ ደም ቀይሕ ለጣላ ክቱብ ሀላ
ተእሪከን።
አግባብ ዐላ መስከብና፡ ብለቅ ዎ ድርቦብ
ሳትርና
ሐን ዕጨዩ ነዓዝል፡ ፍሬሁ ዐላ ሸርፍና
ዳዕር፡ አውሐ ዎ ገርሳ
በለስ፡ ሸግላ ዎ ክስራ
ኢንትረሳዕ ወቀዮ፡ ዐዳይ፡ ነሪድ ዎ ዐቃ።
ምን አልባብና ኢበዴ፡ ንዋይ እታ
መዓጥን
ጌቶት ከደን ንዘከር፡ ነላት ገታእ ሸወክን
እመህሚመ፡ ዛራ ዎ ቀብርወእት
ብሌቃት፡ ዜሮ ዎ አወገት
ፈከን ኢንትረስያ፡ ሐቅፈያና እብ
ምርወት።
ዳፈናሆም ሸገሪት፡ ከፈን ኢኮን ወቅዲት
ህቶም ፍዛ ምን ገብአው፡ ሰላም ነዛላ ወዕሪት

And lived off berries.
Daero, Beles, Garsa.

Who can forget your bed
Of sand and the juicy flesh
Of your prickly pears?

Awhe, Shagla, Kisra,
We lived under your care

And still see your herds grazing
With ostrich and gazelles
In the wild pastures.
Emhamime, Zara
Qabrwaat, we felt secure

Young and brave in your arms,
Fed on your love, and
We still clearly recall
How we chose to bury
Our friends with no ceremony

And no shroud, remembering
Instead they risked their lives
And died for us to have
Peace and stand together
Then and now: positive,

Forgiving and faithful
To the places revealing
Who we are and must
Remember to be.
They showed us destiny.

ኢነብድዮ ለለመድ
ወፋቅ ፍቲ ዎ ረሕመት
ፊና ብዬ አናዲ ኢንትረሳዕ ለሐልፈት።

Mussa Mohammed Adem

The Invincible

Say what you like, but step over the line
And he feels his first scar burning again.
Smell the smoke. He has that true killer look
Because he always sees war – it's ugly,
And dirges play like soundtracks in his head –
Shimber, Hebo, Wazafin – constantly
Making him think, "Encircle, attack, attack . . . ."

He sees enemies like sorghum bending
And breaking, their heads spilling out all red.
Never missing the target, his bullets
Fall like rain hitting the lake, and it floods
As in the days of Noah, only with blood.

Fast and taking too many forms at once,
He's blinding and leaves no time to react –
Like July lightning, thunder, downpours and
Fifty days straight of sandstorms uprooting
Boulders like arrows winging from the bow
Of the hero mercilessly slashing
The tendons, crushing and splashing the marrow.

Like rainy season torrents pounding down
From the highlands with more storms behind them,
He comes to fight, saying "Try and stop me."
He crosses any desert, sets a trap
And waits for the strong to choke on their blood.
Crocodiles run away from his jaws.
He lives according to his law.

ኢልትደከል

ኢትሕመው እት ውዳይ ሐቆ ትወረሳ ለምዕዞን፡
ለቀዳሚሒት ግብእና ትልጌ ህሌት ወተንን፡
ለሞት ለአምር መራራ ሸምበር ሂሮ ወዘፍን፡
ወሐርብ ለአምር በሰሩ ዶል ህጁማት ወከብን፡
ምን ደም ከሲሙ ልትመለእ አሽራም ወለ
ከወክን፡
ክም ለፈሪክ ሐንከለ አስግደቶም ለአዳንን፡
ታክር ቴ ለኩፉ ክማ ዘሀፈት ሸዋንን።

> ለሶብ ኢትአጣንብ ለሀለባልብ ወካትሕ፡
> ክምሰል ዝሳም ዐራት እብ መታዊት
> ራግሕ፡
> ስረፍሪፈት ኤተቢት ዕንታት ዌረት
> ቃጥሕ፡
> እብን ወርወራቴ ለዓጭሞታት ፈናቀሕ፡
> ኮኖት ለሀቴ ደርብያ አፍካክ ትወዴ
> ገረምሕ፡
> ሀለ ክምሰል በዲሩ ህሙል ኢሀለ
> ወጃግሕ፡
> ኢልአተርፍ መውዒታይ ወራር ለእቡ
> ለአትጸበሕ።

ኢልትደከል ውሒዝ ረወሪት ለእበን ወዕጨይ
ለምለማ፡
ለሀርቦ ምኑ እት መዐደይ ለዕራዩ ክምሰል
ትጋየማ፡
እታ ኢልስእዉ ጸንሕ ሰቦት እንዴ ጣየማ፡
እብ ወራር ወዘማቴ ሜራስ አብዕቡ ለታለማ፡
ኢልትከሀል ዋራሁ አስጡር ድቁባም ላሸማ።

ቀዳሚቱ እምር ታ አፈች አለሚት ላጆማ፡
ለእሳ ለአምም ወድያ ለክብድ እንዴ ጨምማ፡
ለሐየት ምን ደከሉ ሸዋሪቡ ሐቆ ተምተማ።
> መንደላይል አወንን ሉዲት ኢኮን ግሙቴ፡
> ጭሩም ሀለ ከፈኑ ለቀርቀፉ ብሶቴ፡

88

Wisdom lets a lion or tiger sleep.
Seeing him, you better stay far away.

Fakes and fanatics may think they're heroes
And pluck a whisker but then, catching fire,
Caught in the eyes where they wanted to play,
They have nowhere to hide and no more to say.

He throws the trees and rocks out of his path
And grabs his weapons – nobody's laughing.
Fields planted thick with mines, impossible
Desert sand and heat, crocodiles swarming
Rivers and gaping valleys in his way
Reveal him close and watching overhead
Before he leaves them choked with too many dead.

The third offensive explodes with sirens
And unrolls black clouds like giant bee hives
Disgorging armies fleeing for their lives,
Out of control, surrounding him like knives
And helplessly knocked away in the swing
Of his crushing sword – his entire flesh
Bloody and broken with wounds and lead as the field

Where he stands unafraid, letting no one
Flee as he fulfills the ancient lines,
Playing and singing them too: history
Repeating itself, prophecy come true
And the clear reality to witness:
Welcome to free Nakfa, Setit and Belessa.

Like thunder and lightning, it surprises
Enemy invaders and ululates
Continually to all who can hear

ሓጥር እና ለቤለ አዜ ልሽመክ ሕርበቱ፣
ምን ሰልፍኩም ትራዩሙ ኢትቅርቦ
አፍያቱ፡፡
ሐሬ ለትዕስ ኢትነፍዕ እናብዕ ወለ ሻሳቱ
እሳታ ምክርና እግላ ጸዐዩት ነማቱ፡፡

ምናታ፣ ለለአትውሕሉ እብ እሳት ሰሳም እንዴ
ትጋረፋ፣
ድመለ አለባ ሰር-ሰሮ ለደም ሐቆ ትጃቀፋ፡፡
አበደን ኢልትደከል ለሰረር ክም ትሳከፋ፣
ውሒዝ እረድቱ ገንዲት ሕመር ሻተፋ፡፡

አተርኤቱ ወዴ ገርገራ አልቃም ሰርሩ፣
እት ቀበታ ገናደል እሳት እንዴ
ትመጮሩ፡፡
ሰራር ባዶብ እብ ካቤቱ ወጀሐሩ፣
ሰራር አብሐሩ ለአልግ ዳይዕ ነብሩ፣
ሰራር ዐስተር ለዐውል እባ ደንበሩ፣
ወሰራር ጃዋት ፋስስ እቱ ለእገሩ፣
ኢትክይዱ ከራዊ ሞዳይ ለሀቱ ለሐድሩ፡፡

ግድም ተማ ለፍጉር ትነቅም ሀሌት ንጋረት፣
ጊመት ሳልሳይ ወራር ተሀብል ሀሌት
ሽግሊለት፡፡
እግልካቱ ኢገሜ እንታ ዳቅብ በዐል ሐለት፣
ስለሉ ሰይፍካ ሐዳ ሐልፈት ደኪለት፡፡
ለአማግ ኢልትደክል ኖሱ ለሕማጦ ቤበራ፣
በዲር ሐልፈት መሰሉ ሐሰት ሚባ
ወበራ፡፡
እት ገሮቡ ለብሳ ባርት ለእባ ጌደራ፣
ለአትሳቅሮ ወበርጆ እንዴ ታክስ ስርራ፣
መረብ ምሳሽ ደግመዩ ታሪክ ደንደን
ወአድሀራ፡፡
ሳቦ ስከይ አለቡ ቀበት ሩከት መዐሉ፣
ሐየት ናቅፋ ወሴቲት ኢልትወረር አሽፋሩ፣
ትሽህድ እግሉ በገሉ ፋርስ ረአስለ ቅታሉ፣
ጆሌል በለሳ ደለአባብ ወሀቱ አስምዕ ዕሳሉ፡፡

90

No matter how much bombing and terror
Our country and its people have to bear.
Since the invincible guards our borders,
No more battles like Adwa can take place here,

Though he has seen plenty dig their own graves
Thinking it could if only they were brave
Enough to face him and die, and they did,
And not until we see the Red Sea dry
Will the verdict be any different.
Adi Hakin, Adi Mirug, Deda,
Bada, the deserts and wadi of Dahlak

And the Gash, tumbling from the highlands
Down where the lions drink after their prey,
Also testify to the gift of life
Or death overflowing and in his hands –
In the end, perhaps, all that he understands,

Taking aim with his spirit and his gun,
Measuring the last breath of anyone
Who forgets him and casts the first stone,
And ready to bear every burden
And horrible fire demanding his blood
Yet strangely leaving the hero happy,
Even when he dies without finding his home.

ዐለም ዲቡ ትፈከረት አበርቁ ወሀዳሩ።

ኢኮን ዘበን አሉላ ለሓልፋ እባ መደቱ፣
ለትዐደየ ሕዓዱ ሰኒ ልደሀር ሕፍረቱ፣
ግሱይ ሀለ እት ሻባይ ሮማይ ታክየት
ብጥረቱ።
በዐል ገደቦ ወ ዕለል ገርብ ምና
ክትፈቱ፣
እትካመታ ረሳሳት ሓቆ ተሓደረት
ቅንቤቱ፣
አረይ ገብአው ወስለብ ረጅፈው ምና
ቃሎቱ።
ይብስት ኢህሌት አዜማ ለበሓር ቆሪ ልገታ፣
ሕሩጥ ሀለ አፍርንጂ እግላ ጅራ ወሳሕታ።
አምዐል ዴዳ ወዶ ወድ ሃኪን ቀጸፋቶም ናተፋ፣
እላ ትገበእ ቀላሉ እት ኢናዩ ለትገሀፋ፣
ዐድ ምሩግ ወ በዳ ደንከል ዲባ ሰቦታ፣
ምንቱ ዲቡ ለአትጋዌሕ ሓባል እንዴ ሻፈታ፣
ጋሽ መስከብ ሓዮት ወአወንን ድርይ ምን ከበሳ።

ቀዳሚቱ ኢዳግም ምስል ሀርማ ለትበአሰ፣
ኩክት አመቃርብቱ ነብየ ምና ግንሓታ።

አታክር እቶም ምን ጅፈር ርሓም አስክ
ተአባጽዕ፣
ልጀርቡ ሕማጥካ ጅልክ ፍትነት ለራቅዕ፣
ለናይ ማሌ ጽዋርካ ስሑል ሀለ ወባቅዕ።
ይእቤላ እብ አተባቃር ወይእቤላ እብ ወገም፣
በዲር ዐለት ወአዜ ሓሰት ኢኮን ወድግም፣
ለዐራቤ ለገሀራ ሃይሞት እንዴ
ትጀማጅም፣
ሓቆሁ በዐል አለባ ለምርወት ምኔት እት
ዓጭም፣
ሀቱ ቱ በዐል ሰልፋ ሰብክ እባ ወ
ሳግም፣
ወ ሀቱ ቱ በዐል አክራ ለአቴ ምስላ
መላግም።

92

Mohammed Said Osman

Juket

Juket broke up with me and left.
I don't know why.
Not enough love? Another guy?
What can I do?

Curse God and die?
I can't get her out of my head.
I feel beat up.
Happiness is being dead

And not in love.
Will she ever want me again?
Maybe one of my poems would make
Juket listen?

Juket, I'm your faithful dog,
On guard and coming when you say.
Tell me to follow and I will,
Only seeing your body sway,
Not caring if my legs fall off.
I'll hold on by your eyelashes
And eyes as sharp as a gazelle's.
Your teeth and smile will bathe my soul
Like milk and keep me out of hell.
Letting your long hair tumble down
Your round breasts to your narrow waist,
You know I'm starving for a taste.
Wine beads the bottle of your neck.

ጁከት!

አስእሲኒ ወጁከት ሻምነ አሬ ትበደለ
በዓል ሻም እለ ኢወዶ አልባብ ሐቆ ተሐበሪ፣
ዐንበልበለ ለልብዬ አስተንተና ወትስእለ፣
አግቡይ እንዶ ለአኖኬ ላሲ ትርሃን ካፈለ።

ህመት በአቱ ለልብዬ እብ ዴሪርኪ ትሰርበበ፣
እንቲ ገአኪ ሀጋይኑ ላሲ ወእምዕለ ተወርበበ።
አዳም ልትሰሐቅ ወዳግም ወህቱ ቡነ ትሪበበ፣
ልብዬ በዐለ አማነት አሰር ቆልኪ ትወረበ።

ተላይ ሻምኪ ገብአኮ እሉ ዓይር ወእፈርር፣
መስከነት ለዕንቼ እኪ እንዶ ትትሐወረር።
ሰአነ ለእግርዬ እኪ ተሌ እብ አሰር
ለግርመትኪ ወጁከት ኢትከለቀተ ምን ጇፈር።

ዕንታት ወድ አሬባይ አስፉር ሸለምለም፣
አንያብ ክዕት መስል ታምም ለአያም።
ረቢ አትሄዴኪ እንዶ አገረም፣
እኪ ለኢሪክብ እት እድንያ ትዘለም።

መቅጠን ወለት ጊዶ ወአክዑብ ሻንን፣
ግሬን እብ መንያቱ ጊማይ ዳንን፣
ልብዬ ስለብከዩ ረቢ ለሀውን፣
ገሮብ ገልፋይ ገብአ ወልብ ተንን።

ስጌዳይኪ ማሪ ብጥረት ዕሬምሬ፣
ዕንታት ለሐበራብር ክም ጆለላ ዘሬ፣
ከፐታይኪ ህልክስ ሕንጁር ለማይ ዳዊ፣
ሻምኪ ወቀጼኒ ገብአ ሕማም በአዊ።

መሌትሐት ሐምላት ወግንቦኪ ደውዬ፣
መሐዊት ስለቅሲቅ ክምስለ ውላድ አውሔ
ትንፈሳይኪ ሸፉ እግል ሕሙም ለአርሔ፣
ኖስኪ አተክርዮ እለ ነፍስ ትትወሐ።

94

It's like a spring I want to drink.
I'm like a wasp, but you're the sting
All the way down, pointing your legs.
A breath of your breath
Will keep me from death
To nibble your cheeks like chocolate cake.
Maybe something like this will bring
My Juket back
And she will sing
I see you suffering. Enough.

If not, I'm stuck
Out in the cold
With no one and nothing to make
Life worth living.

ሐሰብ አቡኪ ቶብ ውደይ ወረሐመት፣
ሽብብ አብሊኒ 'ግል ትትገልጸጽ ለጊመት፡፡
ኢጸበርኩ ረሐመትኪ አኖኬከ. እብ ሀመት፣
እንቲ ምንዲ ኢትሸቢ ኢትሐልፊኒ ዮም ዓመት፡፡

Mohammed Osman Kajerai

Singing Our Way to Victory

Dear friends,
Faithful through the night
I'm back from exile.
With dawn at my door,
The voice of injustice
Doesn't scare me.
I'll make it listen to my gun
And a thousand explosions
Declaring that our struggle
For freedom
Will gleam in the sun
And I will proudly
Witness what I'm made of.
Past the point of anger
As we sing our way to victory,
I can either serve revenge
Calmly and cold,
Crack like lightning and thunder
Across the horizon,
Raining blood to feed the land,
Or I can sow the seeds of hell
So quietly that the prophets can go home.
Even after I die,
My blood and my fire
Will always glow,
Consuming and drowning
Any invader who tries
To waste our fertile land.

لحنُ الانتصارْ

يا رفاقي
ها أنا في ليلي الصامد ودَّعتُ اغترابي
عبثاً يهدر صوتُ البغي ...
ضوء الفجر لن يلبث أن يطرقَ بابي
صوتُ رشاشي ... وكل الانفجاراتِ العنيفه
... كلها تعلن إني أرفض العار وأمشي
في طريق الشمس مرفوع الجبينْ
فأنا خلف براكين الغضبْ
نبضاتُ الثأر ترنيمة شدوي وغنائي
ها أنا أمتد كالعاصفةِ الهوجاءِ في أفق سمائي
أطعمُ الأرض بأشلائي وأسقيها دمائي
نزرعُ الصمتَ جحيماً فاستريحوا أنبيائي
لن يجف الدم لن تنطفئ الشعلة حتى بانتهائي
فإذا ما جاء للأرض غريبْ
يشعلُ النارَ على السهلِ الخصيبْ
كان حتماً أن يلاقي ...
... عاثر الخطو أتوناً من لهيبْ

كان حتماً أن يصيرَ الماءُ
في حُمْرة أذيال المغيبْ
من هنا مرَّ على قلبِ بلادي

98

Crouching in its heart
With dawn beside me
And joining the centuries
Of singing our way to victory
As a people as sure to remain
As the rocks jutting out of the earth
Like the rage pounding in our chests,
I'm ready for the latest enemy
Who wants to dig my grave.
Looking for the moon,
I feel the breeze and rain instead.
It washes our path in the sand
Where, together again dear friends,
I plant the landmines for our struggle
To continue, raising our flag
As the gunpowder explodes
Into fire and smoke –
The valley of death's shadow
Making white mercury purple,
Suffusing the horizon
And lingering in the air like chrysanthemums.
Every rock conceals a freedom fighter.
Our flag rises red with the dawn
And brightens with the day,
Bursting into song the news of victory.

زارعو النار وحفارو القبورْ
روَّعوا ترنيمة الفجر على مرِّ العصورْ
... فتلقاهم خضمُّ الغضبِ الهادرِ منْ كلِّ الصدورْ
غيَّبتهم أرضُنا
لمْ يبقَ إلا شعبنا النابت من صلدِ الصخورْ
... ها أنا أرفع وجهي للقمرْ
لنسيم الغيم ينسابُ رذاذاً ومطرْ
حينما يغسلُ دربي
ها أنا أزرع ألغامي على قلبِ الرمالْ
ومعي كل الرجالْ
نرفعُ الراية في دربِ النضالْ
فإذا هدرَ البارودُ ناراً ودخانْ
وإذا ما رفَّ ظلُّ الموتِ في كل مكانْ
يستعيرُ الزنبقُ الأبيضُ لون الأرجوانْ
يغمرُ الساحة عطرٌ من رياض الأقحوانْ

كلُّ صخرٍ يلتفُّ حوله مناضلْ
وفدائيٌّ مقاتلْ
لترفَّ الرايةُ الحمراءُ
تستقطبُ أضواء النهارْ
ويزف الفجرَ في الساحةِ لحنُ الانتصارْ

Woman of Eritrea

Elegant, exalted and true,
Born of the rock of respect, faith and resistance,
And stepping coolly through the flames of war,
Woman of Eritrea,

Your eyes and all you see
Inspire our struggle endlessly
To reign down terrors like the end of the world
To make the dawn and every day worth living.

Shocked by our naked power,
The horizon roars with our coming together.
Our respect and admiration
Comes with sharing a lifetime of struggle

And even wrapping our wounds in struggle.
To be a martyr for this cause
Is glorious, and goodbyes should not be sad.
But before I disappear

I would ask you to lay my cheek
On the earth as if it were your breast,
Remember me and go with high spirits and passion
To the wounded who continue to share our struggle.

الفتاة الإرتريّة

يا فتاةً في أتون الحرب تخطو
في اعتزازٍ وشموخٍ ووسامه
إنما أنتِ ابنة الصخر صمودا
وإباءً ووفاءً و كرامه
فلعينيكِ تحدينا الأعادي
وصنعنا كلَّ أهوالِ القيامه

كل يومٍ مرَّ من غيرِ كفاحٍ
هو يومٌ ضاعَ من عمرِ الصباح
فتعالي نملأ الأفقَ هديراً
نتحداهُ بأمجادِ السلاح
شاركيني شرفَ العمر جهادًا
ضمدي في ساحةِ الحربِ جراحي

فإذا متُّ شهيداً ودعيني
إنّها لحظة مجدي فذريني
إنها أمنيتي الكبرى دعيني
فوق حضنِ الأرضِ يرتاحُ جبيني
ضمدي جرح رفاقي واذكريني
واصلي جهدكِ في عطفٍ ولين

A Dowry to See Freedom

The most precious dowry I can give,
Dear love, is for you always to see freedom.
Its path will spread before our eyes,
Pull down all the walls of tyranny,

And finally roll out the scroll of our struggle,
Revealing our heroes' sacrifice like thunder
And lightning crashing around our flags
Unfurling over our rocky highlands,

Across the verdant fields of our grain,
Into the bushes, deep in our groves
And echoing like a song: freedom . . .
Echoing from the lonely fortresses

And the hard ground of our struggle in Sawa,
Down to the lake and valleys of El-Kash,
Across the roads of sand to the Red Sea,
Right into the shocking, silver waves

And emerging all over our nation,
Making heroes of us all and our greatest glory,
Free Eritrea, shining in our eyes,
Which any invader without our culture

من أجل عيون الحرية

أغلى ما أملكُ يا قلبي
مهراً لعيون الحريّه
لبلادي في دربِ الأحرارْ
تدكُّ جدار الفاشيّه
ما عادَ كفاحكَ يا وطني
صفحاتُ نضالٍ مطويّه
أبطالكَ في ساحاتِ البذلِ
عواصفُ نار رعديّه
فأرفع راياتكَ يا شعبي
في المرتفعاتِ الصخريّه
في حقلِ الحنطةِ مخّضراً
وعلى الأحراشِ الغابيّه
من (ساوةَ) حيث الأرض
هناك قلاع نضالٍ خلفيّه
في(بَرْكة) في وديان(القاش)
وفي الطرقاتِ الرمليّه
في البحر الأحمر مرهوباً
فوق الأمواج الفضيّه
في كل بقاعكَ يا وطني
يتردد لحنُ الحريّه
من أجلِ العزّة يا شعبي

104

Won't survive, winnowed in shame,
Chaff in the winds of our revolution,
And disappearing like the dust of tyranny
Blown into oblivion.

تَلِدُ الأبطالَ إرتريّة

في أرضكَ ما عاشتْ أبداً

أفواج الغزو الوحشيّه

فهشيمُ الباطل لن يبقى

تذروه رياحُ الثوريّه

Wind and Fire

Victims claim my country as their mother,
Free of humiliation and betrayal
And sacred, yet broken and bleeding –
They greet her with poems, love and flowers.

***

As my blood fertilizes the land,
A mirage of hope gleams on the horizon
Bearing martyrs, martyrs and more martyrs,
But no greater glory or victory. Understand?

***

No more prison, chains, beatings and bleeding
Thanks to the gun giving me the courage
To fight with blazing fire and raging wind
And win, embracing the dawn to fight again.

***

You thugs, invaders, mercenaries –
I'll never stop revenging my land.
Struggle and determination
Define my being Eritrean.

***

The front fighting for my liberation
Pulses through the veins and heart of my song
Unfurling the flag for my martyr's body
To rest and fly in glory forever.

النار والرِّياحْ

يا بلادي أنتِ يا أمَّ الضحايا
اشرف الغدر على ذلِّ النهايه
لكِ مِنْ أقدس أعماق الحنايا
باقة الحبِّ وألوان التحايا

رفرفَ المجدُ على أفق سمائي
حين خضَّبتُ ترابي بدمائي
ورفاقي مِنْ رعيلِ الشهداء
توَّجوا النصر بأمجادِ الفداء

قد تخطيتُ قيودي وجراحي
ببطولاتٍ سلاحي وكفاحي
بلهيبِ النار في هوج الرِّياح
عانقَ النصرُ تباشيرَ الصباح

يا نفايات العصابات الدخيله
لن ينامَ الثأرُ في أرضي القتيله
فأنا أحملُ ميراث الرجوله
ثائرٌ حرٌّ إرتري البطوله

***

108

We unfurl on a hopeless horizon.
We protect you amidst dark days and darker nights.
Your glory in battle and your children
In the struggle and revolution, we provide.

جبهةُ التحرير يا صوت نشيدي
أنتِ في قلبي وفي نبض وريدي

تحت راياتكِ يرتاحُ شهيدي
وعلى دربكِ أمجادُ الخلودِ

نحنُ راياتكِ في أفق المحالْ
نحنُ حراسكِ في ظلم الليالْ
نحنُ أمجادكِ في هول القتالْ
نحنُ ثواركِ أبناءُ النضال

Mohammed Mahmoud El-Sheikh (Madani)

Letter from Aliet

My dear friends,
I've been fighting so long here
That all the birds have died
And my gun has grown into my shoulder.
I sing for all of us denied
Our basic rights and a decent wage.
I won't beg for freedom or stop singing.

We're taking Barentu tonight
And meeting like a groom and bride –
Not with the usual ceremony
But with guns
Singing, bullets for kisses
And shrapnel to caress us
All over our beautiful bodies

Come to the end of brutality
By exploding on top of the enemy.

My dear friends –
No more rooms of our dreams gone up
In the smoke of self-perpetuating
Politicians pretending
They will back our cause.

We'll make it
On our land and for our land:
Sunlight aglow in good work's sweat,
Farmers who wed the art of peace,

111

رسالة من (عليت)

لكم مِنْ جذور المدفع المغروس في كتفِ المغنِّي
حيثُ يشتَّار " الزمجًا" والمواويل أغنِّي
ولأجل العاملِ المحروم في الأرض الغريبه
أرفضُ التوقيع في صكِّ التمنِّي
بل أغنِّي،،
"آه" "بارنتو" نحنُ آتون العشيه
نحن آتونَ لإتمام الزفافْ
حفلنا فيه رصاصْ
والتواقيع التفافْ
والمغنِّي "بندقيه"
والبنياتُ هنا لسنا صبايا
بل شظايا
تسحقُ الظلمَ وتمحو البربر يه
يا رفاقي
لمْ نعدْ تبغا يدخن في دهاليز السياسه
لمْ نعد محض عباءه
يرتديها أخنث قومٍ ليواري ما وراءه
إنما نحن نحن إراده
نحن للأرض ومن الأرض وبالأرض ننادي
نحن للعامل شمسا
نحن للزارع عرسا

112

The wounded under their triumphal arch
And the trigger locked
In the revolution's palm.

ولجرح الشعب في الساحة قوسا
وعلى الكف للثوري زنادا

Singing for the Children of Ar

Singing for the children of Ar
Means surviving the final battle

Singing for the children of Ar
Means epic revelation

Singing for the children of Ar
Means no more talk but action

Yet peace enough to endure
Death stalking Setit on fire
And the songs of love and hate
Bursting from my heart

Listen to these two
Before we reach the sea:

First:
> *I am cactus and sand,*
> *Barren and no rain,*
> *A desert without green.*
> *I am hunger*
> *Eating your land,*
> *Seizing your voice,*
> *Making you bitter*
> *And your only choice*
> *To be a toy of death*
> *Unless you also sing . . . .*

أغنية لأطفال آر

- نذلٌ أن
إنْ متُّ قبل الانفجارْ
- نذلٌ
إذا اختبأتْ حكايةُ أمَّتي خلف الجدارْ
- نذلٌ
إذا اخترتُ التشبثَ بالهتافِ وبالشعارْ

يكفي مهادنة
فالموتُ يرتجُّ من (سيتيت) ناقوساً من اللهبِ
والقلبُ أغنيتان مِنْ حبٍّ ومِنْ غضبِ
بيني وبين البحر أغنيتانْ
أغنيةٌ من الصبّار والرمل الذي يكبرْ
أنا الصحراء لا قطرٌ ولا سُقيا ولا أخضرْ
أنا الجوعُ الذي يجتاحُ عالمكمْ
أُرابيكمْ
أقايضكمْ
ولا مجان عندي غير هذا القبرْ
وأغنية مِن الإمكان للإنسان أن يخّضرْ
" أنا الآتي ...
اليجيءُ ...
يحاصرُ الصحراءْ "

116

Second:

> *Beloved, I return.*
> *I am coming like rain*
> *To children who burn*
> *In a sallow desert.*
> *A flowering cactus*
>
> *Inspires them like the sea*
> *At twilight, stars*
> *Falling into the forest*
> *And the dance of my dagger*
> *Against hunger.*
> *I plow it under*
> *With all our frustration,*
> *And shining deep within*
> *The furrows, written in our blood,*
> *I see victory.*

I know I'm dark and rough,
But two songs are enough
To beat back my fear
Of dying in this war.

When I hear
The children playing the "martyrs and enemies" game –

> *I'm first.*
> *No me.*
> *But you're only three.*
> *The oldest go last.*
> *How about me?*
> *Who will it be?*
> *Hamed. Dabroum.*

يكسرُ لونها الأصفرْ
أنا المطرُ الذي بشتاقه الأطفالْ
يمنحُ شوكة الصبّارْ
لون البحرْ
أنا الشفقُ / الشعاعُ / الانتماءْ
الغابة/ المفتاح/ الخنجرْ
ضدّ الجوعْ
أحملُ معدنَ الإنسان والمحراثِ والدفترْ
ضدّ القهرْ
أكتبُ بالدم الأحمرْ
سأحملُ فوهة البركان حتى النصرْ
لأنّي أشعثٌ أغبرْ

بيني وبين الموت مزموران
تعالوا نلعب الشهداء والعسكرْ
- أنا الأولْ .. -
- أنا الأولْ.. -
- أنا من عمركم أكبرْ -
- أول الأشياء للأصغرْ -
- أنا "حامدْ " -
- أنا" دبرومْ" -
- أنا "جنجرْ" -
" ... ألمْ مسفن وسعديه"

118

Ginger. Alem
Mesfin. Saadiya.
Kabroum. Me!
Me! Me!

– I say, *Quiet! Enough!*
But they talk back. *Now you be the enemy.*
Let's fight!

And I respond.
I can't be the enemy.
They're gone anyway,
And you will stay.
I sing for the children of Ar,
Of a love in the forest and caves
Of Golujj – a painting finished
With the barrel of a gun – the soldier,
Abraham, shot, carrying out the body
Of his hero, Mahmuday.

- أنا "كبروم"
- أ...أ...
كفى يا أخوتي يكفي
تبقّى جانب العسكرْ
- كنِ القائدْ
- لماذا لا تكنْ أنتَ؟
- كنِ القائدْ
- لماذا لا تكن أنتَ؟
- كفى يا صاحبي يكفي
تذكَّر أننا نلعبْ
- فإنَّ زمانهم بائد
ونحن زماننا التالدْ
هو العائدْ
سأرفضُ منصب القائدْ

بيني وبين الحبِّ
هيكل غابةٍ ومغارتانْ
- أنا(قلُوج)
- أنا العشقُ الذي خطَّاه
"أبرا هامْ"
"محموداي"

أسطوره
- أنا اللونُ الذي أكملَ الصوره
- أنا التاريخُ يصنعه رجالٌ خلف ماسوره

120

Children of Ar,
My story won't go away,
For you and for all generations to come.

ستبقى قصتي لكم.. وللأطفالْ
لمُجملِ قادم الأجيالْ
مأثوره
أنا الثوره
أنا الثوره

Abdul Hakim Mahmoud El-Sheikh

Breaths of Saffron on Broken Mirrors

Lust won't leave me alone,
Confused and wanting you
Bathed in juicy colors
As we fall on each other
And I bathe like a hero
In your body full of desire . . .
But it's me hissing
And a little water
Before I'm feeling guilty
Until I see these notes
Echoing outside and not unnatural
But as joy with passion
And turning me upside down,
Oblivious to any niceties
Of the thin water of reason.
I remember love again,
A time to write poetry
Without carving it on my forehead,
When I shun both sides of the river
To look in the mirror of its flowing.
I see love born amidst three stories:
Oleander covering my face;
Writing I see on the feet
Of some poor farmers walking by;
And how the peace we found in trees
Filled us so deeply
That we discovered the power of revolution.
Can you imagine my fascination

المرايا والحكايا وانبعاث الزعفرانْ

مسكونٌ بجفاء الرغبه

اشتاقكَ مختارا

والرؤية تختار الألوان البدويه

متكئاً منهارا

والروعة في روعتها تتدثرُ

بالماء الآخذِ في استمنائي

وفحيحُ الأوزار المستوطنِ في ذاتي

يتماوجُ خلف النافذة

يؤنسنُ عشقي/ يقصد رشقي

يربكُ كل تفاصيل حبيبتكِ المائية يا زمني

زمنُ الشِّعرِ أشاحَ بوجهِ النّهرْ

تموضعَ فيض مرايا

أودعَ سُررَ المعدنِ آيه

أزاولُ مهدَ العشقِ حكايه

يسقطُ وجهي سحباً دفلى

رهطُ حفاةٍ فلاحينْ

بقايا شجرٍ أيقظ فينا بوحَ الثورة بالإمكانْ

وبوناً كادَ ... وعادَ

وشادَ حنينا ألبَّ عشقي ضدَّ مروجي

شرخ شخوصي لغةً تعزف عينا

ولداً يترقبُ إيماضَ سراويلَ القمح

يهمهمُ بالسرو نشيداً

نكداً يتدلى مِنْ بين الأغصانْ

124

When birdsong attacked a meadow
That bloomed only for my eyes
Before my own tongue took over
Prophesying a newborn amidst the sheaves
Of wheat in the gleam of harvest?
And why *this* chant sulking in the cypress
Before tumbling through the branches
And overpowering a man
Known as a lily in the field?
Like henna lines we surrounded him
Before a dream vision
Of strong language like radiation
Repelling love in action
Required a heart to heart conversation.
Before I was so angry
I was smoother than a lentil
And full of nurture overflowing
For a thousand wounded,
Another thousand dead,
And one particular woman
Passing away forever to that far shore
Between my wanting and leaving her.
Listen. From now on,
Never will I waste another day,
Never, even if I have no poetry,
Even if I reject every single word,
Never again will I waste a single day –
At least not as long as I love
To see her smile so clearly
And find her body's wild curves
In the waves crashing to shore
For a song of our martyrs' remains.

وتهزمه سوسنةٌ في الحقلِ
ننداحُ بأوردةِ الليمونِ حنايا
ماذا" فيني" خلف عيوني؟؟!
أقوى لغة تكتسح فعل الحبِّ
وترشحُ حتى يندى قلبُ القلبِ
ماذا عنّي قبل جنوني
أسوى حبّةِ عدسٍ طفحتْ
تُرضعُ ألفَ جريحٍ
ألفَ قتيلْ
أهوى امرأة كنتُ أراوحُ

"بين هروبي منها والخفقانْ"
صرتُ أصرخ أنّي
لن أتنازلَ عن أيامي القادمة
لو اطلقني الشّعر
وطلّقتُ الكلماتِ
لن أتنازلَ حتى
لن أتنازلَ حتى
لن أتنازلَ عنها
يا امرأتي الواضحة البسماتِ
الفاضحة القسماتِ
تدويرُ القولْ
هديرُ البحرْ
تتناغمُ أشلاء الشهداء

Ahmed Mohammed Saad

For the Tired

For the tired
For the adoring
For our children
Stranded outside

     For the road builders
     At the dawn of our epic sacrifice
     My flag will always fly

     Freedom and my country
     Make me love who I am

Dear friends, I burn like a torch,
Yearning to be close
And wrapped in your arms
With my flag on its lance
Flying for you
And always high
Amidst the harmony
And pulse of your voices

My freedom and my country
Make me love who I am
Pulling down the walls
And letting go of all the misery
We have suffered for too long
To shine brightly
As the cause of our revolution
Fearing no one

من أجل من ذاقَ الضنا

مِنْ أجلِ مَنْ ذاقِ الضنا
مِنْ أجلِ مَنْ عشقَ السنا
مِنْ أجلِ أطفالٍ لنا
قد شُردوا خلفَ العراءْ
مِنْ أجلِ من شقُّوا الطريقَ
وشيدوا فجر الملاحم والفداءْ
سأظلُّ أرفعُ رايتي
أنِّي أريدُ هويتي
حريِّتي ... جنسيتي...
يا رفاقي مازلتُ أسمع صوتكمْ متناغماً في داخلي
ما زلتُ أسمعُ نبضكمْ
لحناً يعانقُ خافقي وسنابلي
ما زالَ يجرفني الحنين لقربكمْ
صارَ الحنينُ مشاعلي
مِنْ أجلكمْ يا أخوتي
سأظلُّ أرفعُ رايتي
أنِّي أريد هويتي
حريِّتي
جنسيتي
فليسقط البؤسُ الذي
سحقَ الجموعَ مدى السنينْ

128

And unrelenting
In resistance and marching
Faithfully to join
In building the road
Of our glory in a dawn
Without the pain
Of humiliation, prison and chains

لن تحبسَ الجدرانُ نور قضيتي

لا لنْ أهابَ مِن الطغاةِ العاصبينْ
* * *
أبدًا تشق مبادئي مجدي
إلى الفجر المبينْ
بالزحفِ والعزم الذي لا ينثني
... سأحطمُ الأغلالَ
والسجن المهينْ

Ahmed Omer Sheikh

A Song from the Coast

Listen closely. Look up.
Do you hallucinate
That the stars are dropping
Out of the pockets of the night

Or that your rage
Upsets the universe?
Thinning like clouds, we age
And die before we see

Beyond the threshold
Contained in stanzas
Of a poem so bold
It reels hearing the hum

Of the gleaming stars
Coursing in its blood.
But if I could see more,
Let it be my country!

Or am I dreaming?
Is it nothing
But wind in a palm tree –
Restless, stirring, wandering

And lost in the wilderness?
Is even the threshold
Of a future for my country
Just another hallucination?

أنشوده ساحليه

اقترّبْ
فالليالي تتيهُ على منكبيها الشّهبْ
والرؤى واهمه
ازرع الهمَّ وأمضِ بدربِ الغَضَبْ
أنَّها الخاتِمه
تستطيلُ بقاماتنا والسُّحبْ
فالوصيد الوصيدْ
اشتعلْ عبر بهو القصيدْ
تهادَ على هَمْهَماتِ الوريدْ
إنَّها الخطوةُ القادِمه
فاسكب العزمَ يورقُ حلمٌ جديدْ
أيُّها الأسمرُ المتلألئُ عبر الفضاءِ النشيدْ

(سادتي سيداتي)
هنالكَ حيث الهوى يستفيقْ
نوغلُ عبر زوايا الحريقْ
تدقُ دفوفُ الوطنْ
وانتفاض الزمنْ

(سادتي)

كان لي أنجمٌ ومحارْ

132

Keep going. Let the rage
Burn through your wounds.
Fight for what you've lost
And find the voice to bring it back.

بلادٌ كلؤلؤةٍ ساحليه
أنشودةٌ وطنيه
تخبِّئها جنياتُ البحارْ
نهرٌ يفيضُ بحبِّ الصّغارْ

وطني أيُّها الانتماءْ
أيِّ سهدٍ يورِّقُ همَّ النخيلْ
إنّه المستحيلْ
يترنحُ عبر فيافي الرحيلْ

وطني أيُّها الكبرياءْ
أيُّ طفلٍ يغوصُ ببحرِ العراءْ
والرؤى واهمه
أيها المرتقب

أرحل الآن عبر اشتعال الغضبْ
تستطيلُ على عربداتِ الجراحْ
" السلاحُ السلاحْ "
يستعادُ الحِمى
والديارُ تموجُ على عتباتِ النواحْ

أيُّها المستباحْ
إنّها الخاتِمه
فازرع الهمَّ وأمضِ بدربِ الصّباحْ

134

About the Poets and Poems

Meles Negusse (1975): Poet and journalist. Nominee of the 2001 Raimok competition, Eritrea's highest award for literature, for his writing in Tigrinya, he studies psychology at the University of Asmara. "Mammet" first appeared in 2000 and "Wild Animals" in 1997. Both are from an unpublished book of poetry.

Isayas Tsegai (1956): Poet, songwriter and theatre specialist. M.A. in Theatre Studies from Leeds University, he is the director of the Sewit Children's Theatre and has been instrumental in the development of Eritrean theatre in general. "I Am Also a Person" first appeared in 1989 and "Lamentation" in 1995. Both are from his book, *Lemin-Leminey* (1998).

Solomon Tsehaye (1956): Poet and critic. Author of Eritrea's national anthem and a coordinator of many Eritrean cultural projects, he has served as Director of the Cultural Affairs Bureau in Eritrea's Ministry of Education. "The Tithe of War" is from his book, *Sahel* (1994).

Angessom Isaak (1963): Poet and short story writer. Public relations and coordinating officer at the Cultural Affairs Bureau of the PFDJ, he has published three books: *Sewerti Biet Mahbus* (1987), *Belay Shida* (1992) and *Zinededet Kara* (with Michael Berhe and Ghirmai Yohannes) (2000). "Freedom's Colors" first appeared in 1996 and is from an unpublished book of poetry.

Fessahazion Michael (1954-1980): Poet and journalist. Member of the editorial board of *Gedli Hizbi Ertra*, the official monthly periodical of the ELF (Eritrean Liberation Front) in the mid-

135

1970s, he died in action during Eritrea's war of independence. "Naqra" is from *Gedli Hizbi Ertra* No. 6 (1 January 1976).

Ribka Sibhatu (1956): Poet, critic and scholar. Intercultural consultant in Italy with a Ph.D. in Communication Studies from the University of Rome, she writes poetry in Tigrinya and in Italian. "Abeba" is from her bilingual book, *Aulò: Canto-poesia dall'Eritrea* (1993).

Saba Kidane (1978): Poet, performer and journalist. Presenter and coordinator of broadcasts on Eritrean television and radio, she also writes for newspapers. "Growing Up" (2001), "Go Crazy Over Me" (2001) and "Your Father" (1999) are from an unpublished book of poetry.

Beyene Hailemariam (1955): Poet and critic. Italian educated, M.A. in sociology and a prisoner of war for nine years in Addis Ababa, where he wrote some of his poetry, he publishes his work sparingly. "Silas," "Let's Divorce and Get Married Again" and "For Twenty Nakfa" — all first published in 2000 — are from an unpublished book of poetry.

Fessehaye Yohannes (1958): Playwright and journalist. Written in 1988, "If He Came Back" is from *Mezmur Tegadaly* (1992), edited by Ghirmai Ghebremeskel.

Reesom Haile (1946 – 2003): Poet and scholar. Ph.D. in Media & Communication and Eritrea's best known poet in the west, he returned to Eritrea in 1994 after exile which included teaching and lecturing in western universities and working for international NGOs. His first collection of Tigrinya poetry, *Waza ms Qum Neger nTensae Hager*, won the 1998 Raimok prize. His other books of poetry include *We Have Our Voice* (2000) and *We Invented the Wheel* (2002). "Voice" and "We Have" are from *We Have Our Voice*.

Ghirmai Ghebremeskel (1948): Writer and critic. Editor of *Mezmur Tegadalay* (1992), the first anthology ever published of

Eritrean poetry, he wrote extensively during the independence struggle and after and is Chief Executive of the Eritrean Civil Service Administration (CSA). "A Candle for the Darkness" first appeared in 1988 and is from the same anthology.

Fortuna Ghebreghiorgis (1978): Poet. "Help Us Agree" (2001) is from an unpublished book of poetry.

Solomon Drar (1956): Novelist, historian and poet. M.A. in Theatre Studies from Leeds University, he is the director of Hdri Publishers. His books include two novels – *Mekete* (*Challenge*: originally written in 1988, published in Asmara in 1992) and *Echa Hanti Sidra* (*A Family's Destiny*, 1994) – and a historical work, *Eritrawiyan Kommando: Qiya 18 Deqayiq* (*Eritrean Commandos: A Legend of 18 Minutes*, 1996). "Who Said Merhawi Is Dead?" is from the anthology, *Mezmur Tegadalay*.

Ghirmai Yohannes (San Diego) (1961): Actor, poet and writer. His work includes television shows, children's programs, videos, advertising, stand-up comedy and theatre. "Like a Sheep" and "Next Time Ask" first appeared in 1997, "Unjust Praise" in 1994, and "Who Needs a Story?" in 1996.

Paulos Netabay (1967): Journalist, poet and songwriter. He is editor-in-chief of *Haddas Ertra*, Eritrea's national, Tigrinya newspaper. "Remembering Sahel" first appeared in 1995.

Mussa Mohammed Adem (1963): Poet, short story writer and journalist. He has worked in Tigre radio broadcasting since 1992.

Mohammed Said Osman (1967): Poet and journalist. Head of the Program Development Unit for Educational Mass Media at the Ministry of Education, he won the Raimok prize for Tigre literature in 1995 and wrote "Juket" in 2000. He is the author of *Atrafie Wo Neweshi* (*My Environment and Myself*, 2003), a children's book in Tigre.

Mohammed Osman Kajerai (192? – 2003): Poet. Leading poet and intellectual figure of Eritrea, Sudan and the Arab world, he lived and worked in the Sudan for most of his life. Returning to Eritrea after its independence, he worked briefly in Asmara as a teacher and journalist. His poems are from *Al-Taranim Al Sawyriya* (1984), published by the Association of Eritrean Teachers.

Mohammed Mahmoud El-Sheikh (Madani) (1955): Poet and journalist. Well-known in Sudan and the Middle East, he lives in Saudi Arabia. Both poems are from *Al-Taranim Al Sawyriya* (1984).

Abdul Hakim Mahmoud El-Sheikh (1966 – 1998): Poet and journalist. Mohammad Madani's younger brother, he won Eritrea's prize for Arabic poetry in 1992. At the height of his career, he died in a fire in 1998. "Breaths of Saffron on Broken Mirrors" was first published in 1994.

Ahmed Mohammed Saad (1945-1978): Poet. Recognized as the first serious Eritrean poet in Arabic, he worked briefly in Libya after finishing a degree in agricultural engineering at Cairo University. He died in a car accident. "For the Tired" is from a collection of his poetry and plays, *Asheq Eritrea*, published posthumously in Beirut in the 1980s.

Ahmed Omer Sheikh (1966): Poet, novelist and journalist. With a degree in Economics and Public Administration from King Abdulaziz University, Saudi Arabia, he has worked in the Arabic section of Eritrean radio and television since 1992. Author of three novels – *Nurai* (1997), *Alashria* (1999) and *Ahzan Almatar* (2001) – and three books of poetry – *Heen lem Yaad Algareeb* (1993), *Tefaseel Emrah Khadima mien Alsudan* (1994) and *Rakset Alteyour* (2003) – he has won many national and international prizes, including the Raimok award for Arabic literature in 1995 and 1997. The poem "A Song from the Coast," which first appeared in 1989, is from his first poetry book, *Heen lem Yaad Algareeb*.